'Some believe it is only great power
that can hold evil in check. But that is not
what I have found. I have found that it is
the small everyday deeds of ordinary folk
that keep the darkness at bay. Small acts
of kindness and love'

Gandalf, The Hobbit

MIRROR BOOKS

A huge thanks to all those who helped along the way with the information that made this book possible. None of you can be named but you know who you are and I am hugely grateful for everything you do. Thanks to Kevin and Ernie for the long hours and all the photos. Also to my publishers Mirror Books for their on-going support and valued help and advice.

Nicola Tallant, August 2021

1

Hardback ISBN: 9781913406653
eBook ISBN: 9781913406646

CLASH OF THE CLANS

CLASH OF THE CLANS

BY THE No1 BESTSELLING AUTHOR

NICOLA TALLANT

THE RISE OF THE IRISH NARCOS AND BOXING'S DIRTY SECRET

MIRROR BOOKS

About the Author

Nicola Tallant is the foremost authority on gangland crime in Ireland and holds an H Dip in Criminology.

A journalist for 25 years, she is three times winner of the prestigious *Newsbrands Crime Journalist of the Year Award* and is a regular contributor to television and radio programmes where she is called upon for her expertise about organised crime. She is the host of the *Crime World* podcast and presents and produces TV documentaries.

Nicola is the author of a number of books about crime including the bestseller *The Witness*. She was an executive producer on the podcast *The Witness: In his Own Words* which has topped the charts in Ireland, the UK and Australia.

Contents

1

Double Grey

It was September 2015 and outside the city was just beginning to wake. I had spent the night tossing and turning, with one eye on the neon numbers on the clock beside my bed while my brain dished out warnings to my body ordering it to relax and sleep. It was always that way when I had an early flight to catch, no matter how many times I travelled. And of course I made it. As I always did. With plenty of time.

Time to buy a sandwich. Those 7am flights are great when you actually get there and are standing at the gate ready to depart, a whole day ahead of you at your destination and a sense of smugness about those still in bed just fumbling for a snooze button.

The Dublin to Malaga flight on Aer Lingus is pretty much always full even during the winter months. My fellow passengers were mainly older couples, no doubt heading out to their villas or apartments on the Costa, where they would bask under the Spanish sun in resorts quieter now that the summer tourists had packed up and left. I wandered over towards the kiosk that sold paninis in plastic, large blue muffins in cellophane packaging and sandwiches in triangular boxes. Everyone looked bored, as people do in airports. I picked up a cheese and ham on brown bread. It looked very unappetising but would do. Two coffees. One black. One latte. The photographer was grateful as he saw me wandering back towards our seats with one in each hand. His giant backpack was heavy, filled with cameras, back-up batteries, wide angle and long lenses, tripods and lighting equipment – and he would have foregone the coffee rather than lug it up the terminal to the shop.

"Thanks."

We didn't need to do small talk. We were well used to one another's company. We were used to waiting. Sitting. Watching. To long silences. We had soldiered together long enough.

I must have shifted in my seat. Probably to pick through my handbag for the umpteenth time. At the departure gate something caught my eye. Familiar. Out of place here in this sea of ordinary. Double grey. And then leather. Chocolate brown. I turned my head. A queue had started to gather at the Gold Circle Line for the Business Class passengers. There were a few men in smart casual with briefcases, a woman in a sharp business suit, a smattering of well-to-do couples with matching designer carry-on luggage and then there were the three.

They came into my vision all together. The burly beefcake with the orange skin squeezing the zips of his Canada Goose jacket, the girl with the brown hair and impossibly long pink acrylic nails and the other guy in a grey tracksuit, wearing a baseball cap pulled right down over his eyes. The Louis Vuitton bag at his feet. Chocolate brown. I looked harder and could see the huge gold watch weighing heavy on his wrist. The cap was Hugo Boss. He looked up. We locked eyes. I held my ground. Daniel Kinahan, the boss of the largest organised drug gang to ever come out of Ireland, knew me and I knew him. I'd been writing about him for years. I was standing in an airport with a coffee in a cardboard cup *because* of him. And we were about to board a flight together to Spain, to the seat of his power and to the place where his one-time best friend had just been shot dead, left in a pool of blood on a pavement at the prime of his life. The murder of Gary Hutch just 24 hours previously had shaken the foundations of the Irish criminal underworld. Not only had Hutch been a senior lieutenant in the Irish mafia but he was also the nephew of the legendary Gerry 'The Monk' Hutch.

The announcement that we were boarding was shrill. Kinahan grinned and picked up his bag, probably worth more than I would earn on my mission to find out what had happened to Hutch. His giant Rolex watch could probably pay my salary for a whole year. That's drug money for you. I waited as the Gold Circle passengers were called to board. Kinahan and his pals elbowed their way to the front. He was nothing like his father. He didn't look like an international businessman. He looked like a drug dealer in double grey.

As we flew 30,000 feet over France and on towards Spain I chewed on the ham and cheese sandwich and pondered. I know that organised crime is a violent and a ruthless world, I write about it all the time. But surely Kinahan couldn't have been feeling too good. The callous and cold assassination of Hutch, his one-time wingman, must have been weighing on him. I couldn't restrain my curiosity much longer and I certainly wasn't in any mood to doze. I unlocked my seatbelt and shuffled past the photographer who raised an eyebrow to me in warning as I indicated I was just needing the bathroom.

At the entrance to first class, opposite the doors of the toilets, I started to stretch my legs and looked around to make sure nobody was watching. The passengers' heads nodded from side to side. Some slept on travel pillows, others were lost in books. I pulled back the curtain just enough to see in and scanned the backs of the huge armchairs. I spotted the unmistakable balding head of the son and heir of the Kinahans' estimated £1 billion drug fortune. He was lying back, shoes off, feet up and busy on his mobile phone. The baseball cap was in his hand ready at all times to be placed back on his head, a comfort blanket of sorts.

He and Gary Hutch had been inseparable once. They'd shared everything from prostitutes to a rented villa in their adopted home in southern Spain, where every ambitious gangster goes to graduate. They were part of a club, a brat pack and later a mob which rivalled the mafias on the Costa Del Crime.

I'd met plenty of criminals in my time and found that many of them were decent underneath a hard exterior, some just wanted to provide for their families the only way they knew how. But the Kinahan crew were different. Ruthless. Cruel. Immoral. And Hutch had been one of them, so trusted in the belly of the Kinahan organisation that when the Irish mafia decided to finish with Dublin hitman Paddy Doyle, years previously, it was he who had lured his childhood pal into the trap. Hutch had escaped unharmed when their Jeep came under attack – because that was the plan. Doyle had died and Hutch had returned to Dublin to carry his coffin and claim to his parents that the Russians were to blame.

To nail down the pretence, Daniel Kinahan had offered the money to pay for the funeral. Hutch was no saint. He'd lived by the sword and he died by the sword. That he had likely suffered the same fate, the same type of double cross at the hands of his own, was pretty clear. But his death wouldn't be forgotten like Doyle's. His would be avenged. There was no doubt. The ins and outs of what had happened lay somewhere out there in Spain.

In front of me, Kinahan looked like the cat who had got the cream. Comfortable in his mile-high alibi it seemed to me that death, just like his seat, was simply business.

The plane landed and quickly the Business Class passengers were allowed to disembark as the rest of us remained in our seats so as not to get in their way. There is something quite grounding about that class structure that exists on planes. You get what you pay for. You pay for what you can afford and your fellow passengers can read and judge you accordingly. They left quickly, one after the other. First off was double grey. The brown leather bag swung at his side. The hat was back on his head. I wanted to see how he left the airport, although I knew he would probably be long gone by the time those of us in economy were allowed to disembark.

The bag with the cameras was awkward but we were glad we hadn't put it in the hold. We walked as fast as we could without running to passport control and onwards to the arrivals area, where I just caught a flash of the bag, the grey tracksuit bottoms, across the hall at a stairwell. The beefcake and the girl were gone but there was another guy with him now. He looked Spanish, maybe, dark. They both had their phones in their hands and they were looking back towards me. I turned my head back to arrivals and dramatically looked at my watch, then up to the screens above, which announced the times of flights landing into Malaga from all over the world. The photographer kept an eye. He watched them watching me. The Spaniard took Kinahan's bag and gave him a shoulder hug. They laughed. And then they jogged up the steps and out into the Spanish sun. We waited for a while, wandering around the airport and doubling back on ourselves a few times to make sure we weren't being followed. We'd been here before and we knew all about the Kinahan spotters and if we were going to get any work done at all we certainly didn't want company.

Later, we made our way down the coast and found the Angel de Miraflores complex where Gary Hutch had met his end on a Thursday morning.

Discarded crime scene tape fluttered in the breeze but the investigators were gone and all that was left were the tiny hints of the horror that had occurred. We mooched around the dark and lonely car park underneath the complex of apartments where a gunman had waited for the 34-year-old to step outside into the blazing sun. We followed the path around the shared swimming pool where Hutch had run for his life, his killer in hot pursuit firing again and again. We saw the gate he had been trying to get to as, one by one, the bullets came. We stopped at the spot where it had ended, where he was when the eighth bullet ripped through the back of his head.

Ex-pat pensioners had fled and shut their doors as the terrible noises began. What else could they have done? No human is a match for a gun. Reluctantly, they told me of what had happened, how the gunman had run to a getaway car waiting on the road above. How he had got tired halfway up the hill and started to casually walk. How he had let himself out through the electric gates and had left in what looked like a waiting BMW car. Some had got pictures on their phones while the ambulances were called and later when the Guardia Civil made their marks around his body and circled the bullet holes and casings nearby. "They sold theirs to the Sun newspaper... disgusting," one woman whispered as she nodded to a balcony nearby. A couple peered down through the foliage. Nobody knew Gary Hutch or anything about him. He had clearly kept himself to himself in the time he was living in the complex. It was nice but pretty basic, a far cry from the villa he had once shared with Daniel Kinahan. That evening we spoke with contacts who told us that Gary deserved to die. "He was a rat," they said.

I wondered what had happened to the deal I had heard that his uncle, the legendary criminal known as The Monk, had forged with Kinahan's father, The Dapper Don. The offspring may have fallen out but the Godfathers had stepped in, or so we had been led to believe. The story had been like a game of Chinese whispers since it first emerged in Dublin. There were allegations of police being tipped off about drug shipments, of routes into the UK being busted by cops and of Gary Hutch being tested with false information. There was a bank robbery, a pyramid scheme and deals with the Russians. Some said €100,000 had been paid for peace, many said twice that while others said no money had changed hands at all. There were reports of punishment shootings, intimidation and double crosses. Most people I asked seemed to have their own theory, but one thing that everyone agreed on was the terrifying possibilities of a fallout between two powerful criminal families like the Hutch and the Kinahan clans – which had the propensity to divide a city, have ripple effects across Europe and punch right into the heart of professional boxing. This was the proverbial story with legs, the train to God knows where and, as I contemplated what the future would hold, I realised I was already aboard.

2

A Monk and a Dapper Don

It would be hard to find two more different creatures of the underworld than Gerry 'The Monk' Hutch and Christy 'Dapper Don' Kinahan.

One had built his entire reputation on being anti-drugs while the other had become the most significant player on the international narcotics scene that Ireland had ever produced. The Monk insisted he hated all drugs but particularly heroin, a poison that had destroyed his own north inner-city community and the lives of many who had grown up there. Kinahan, on the other hand, had built his foundations on 'smack', the term Dubliners used for heroin. But the differences ran deeper than that and, if the truth be told, The Dapper Don was a middle-class misfit who was out of place in Dublin's traditional criminal underworld. A picture of him dressed in white trousers and a crisp linen shirt with a panama hat in his hand probably embodied everything The Monk and his ilk hated.

The Monk had never intended to become a celebrity. It had

9

come as a result of his success and steely determination to win at life, despite the lousy hand of cards he had been dealt. Gerry Hutch had been born the youngest of eight in the early 1960s and was reared in abject poverty. There had been jobs once, at the dockyards, for the families who squeezed into tiny flats in the rundown Georgian properties that lined Dublin's streets. His own father, Patrick, had once earned an honest wage, while his mother Julia stayed home to mind her brood.

They had little, but it was a proud community and generations of fathers had left for work every morning and returned at night with money to feed their children, but by the time Gerry and his siblings were growing up that had all changed. With the jobs gone, a life on a dole queue was all that awaited the next generation, so Hutch had decided to change life's plan for himself.

He began his own criminal career at the age of 10 and later led the 'Bugsy Malones', a group of hungry and feral inner-city youngsters nicknamed after the hit gangster comedy movie. They were notorious for robbing cash from banks, post offices and even shops throughout Dublin by vaulting the counters and running like hell. They terrorised the city with their multi-pronged arson attacks, robberies and smuggling. Hutch hated the law, politicians and the establishment who sought to bring him to heel as he amassed a string of convictions. Before he knew it, he was in Mountjoy Jail, where he got his degree in crime and found mentors to help him on the road to the big time.

In prison he had become very serious, so much so that he earned his nickname 'The Monk' from fellow lags. In later years, when the media reported that his name represented his no smoking, no drinking attitude to life he went along with it, albeit while laughing into his pint.

He was released in 1985 and within two years was suspected of having orchestrated his first spectacular heist while still in his early 20s. As he basked in his newfound fame and set about making his money grow, Hutch began to detest smack dealers. All around him was the destruction of a heroin epidemic which had hit his north inner-city home harder than anywhere else. There were task forces, Concerned Parents and swathes of community workers, but heroin was bigger than them all and it ate away at the heart and soul of the community.

The Provisional IRA were hugely active at the time and Hutch admired and respected them, but more for their brawn than their politics. He learned very quickly to share his spoils with them, keep them onside and cultivate an image for himself as a Robin Hood-style character who would steal from the rich but who would often help out the poor. The reality was far less heroic and gardai believe that at least some money stolen in the daring robberies was invested in cannabis which was sold around Dublin for large profits. Like all good mafia Dons, Hutch washed his money through the construction industry and bought up cheap properties around the area and beyond. His black hair and icy blue eyes made him stand out on the streets where he would often be seen whispering to underlings or eyeing up passing strangers with suspicion.

The north inner-city was his turf, Dublin was his town and his ability to outsmart police and politicians became legendary. While his brothers Eddie, Johnny, Patsy and Derek stayed living in the area and reared their own families there, Hutch moved out to a middle-class suburb and sent his children to private schools. Unlike him, many of his family lived chaotic lives. Derek was a convicted rapist with a rap sheet for drugs and assault offences. He ended up taking his own life after telling psychiatrists he felt guilty about things he had done in his past. Eddie, a taxi driver, was a blagger who was involved in shoplifting and small-time fraud. He had five children and lived at Poplar Row in the heart of the family territory, while Patsy, a carpet fitter, also lived nearby. Some of their offspring had followed The Monk into armed robbery while others just lived quiet lives in their concrete heartland between the capital's main O'Connell Street and east towards the mouth of the Liffey.

There were many reasons that the likes of The Monk were lawbreakers. For a community already marginalised, the development of the International Financial Services Centre on its doorstep only served as a reminder of how great the divide between the rich and poor was. All around glass towers, private apartments and one million square foot of office space popped up. Banks, multi-national companies and others tempted by the beneficial tax laws brought in by the government moved in in their droves, while a young and well-educated workforce reared outside the area landed well-paid jobs. Promises of investment in the communities affected by the construction work went unkept and for many young people, like some members of the vast Hutch clan, the only clear future was in the drug trade.

All the while, The Monk's star rose, as did his ability to remain one step ahead of the law, due in no small part to the fact that he avoided feuds.

In 1995, when he was suspected of being behind a £3

million robbery at Clonshaugh at a cash holding facility, he cemented his reputation as being a mastermind criminal by planning the heist with military precision. The money, it was suspected, was invested again and eventually ended up in his vast property portfolio and business interests across Ireland, the UK and Europe.

A year later the actions of another criminal, 'Factory' John Gilligan, would change the relatively 'innocent' face of organised crime in Ireland. Gilligan, a pint-sized thug from Ballyfermot, had once worked as a merchant seaman but quickly found that crime was much more lucrative.

He'd earned his nickname by targeting factories in armed robberies and stealing anything he could flog on. But after a stint in prison in the early 1990s he'd discovered that drugs were even more lucrative and less labour intensive. On his release he'd secured a loan, bought his first consignment of cannabis from Amsterdam and never looked back. Within two years he'd amassed an estimated €20 million fortune, bought a large property in the Kildare countryside and built a huge top-of-the-range equestrian centre.

His meteoric rise from working-class criminal to Lord of the Manor had not gone unnoticed and he'd come onto the radar of the country's top crime journalist, Veronica Guerin. She'd written about Gilligan and later called on him at his isolated home where he had viciously assaulted her and threatened to rape her child. Guerin filed a garda complaint. Gilligan was facing serious charges and potentially the loss of his empire, when he decided to murder her on the Naas Road as she sat in her red sports car.

For years The Monk and other big leaguers like George 'The

Penguin' Mitchell and Martin 'The General' Cahill had run rings around the gardai, having fun while doing so. Cahill's murder in 1994 had come at the height of his fame and just three years later, a movie about his life starring Brendan Gleeson and Jon Voight was released to huge acclaim.

For the A-listers the thrill of carrying out robberies, raids and cash grabs had been equalled only by getting away with it and seeing the frustration of the authorities. To them it was the two fingers back to the same middle-class institutions that had expected them to crawl through each day, grateful for whatever scrap was thrown at them. But when Guerin was shot dead, Hutch knew their antics would no longer be tolerated, and that the underworld was going to feel the full force of the state. Calls for crackdowns on crime were already being made, as the nation watched in disbelief when officers dragged tarpaulin over Guerin's car, which had stopped at traffic lights when the ambush occurred. The Monk queued with hordes of mourners to sign a book of condolence at the offices of the *Sunday Independent*, where she had blazed a trail with her reports on organised criminals such as Gilligan – and himself. He wanted the country to know he wasn't like Gilligan, he was disgusted too.

The Criminal Assets Bureau (CAB) was set up in the wake of the murder, under draconian legislation that was swiftly passed through Dáil Eireann. It came like a hammer blow to gangland. The Monk had hoped that they'd go after the drug dealers, but they came at him too and went for the jugular, threatening to take his family home in Clontarf in lieu of tax and interest they said he owed. He was furious and vowed to fight back and ridicule the authorities as he did.

In 1998 he bought a building at Buckingham Street and opened up a boxing club, which he called Corinthians. Boxing had been his life-long passion and his club became a hub for north inner-city fighters and a HQ of sorts for The Monk. Film director Jim Sheridan, who had just shot to fame with his movie The Boxer, starring Daniel Day Lewis, loved the addition to his old neighbourhood and donated a training ring, affording huge recognition for the club. With Hutch as treasurer, Corinthians were given a 99-year lease on the premises, but a High Court case brought about by CAB proceedings saw him named as the mastermind behind the Marino and Clonshaugh robberies, sending the media into a frenzy. He eventually settled with the CAB to the tune of £1.2 million by selling a number of properties and paying the remainder in cash, much of which was delivered damp to Bureau officers.

For someone so proud, the public ridiculing by the CAB had made him even more determined to take back his reputation as an untouchable crime boss. A year after he'd been forced to pay up, he went to court and was granted a taxi driver's licence, as the settlement of the CAB bill had also proved that he was then tax compliant. He set up a limousine service dubbed 'Carry Any Body', a pun on the Bureau and over the proceeding years he dressed up as a chauffeur and drove around the city centre, telling anyone who would listen that he was broke and had to make an honest living. Punters queued to have their photographs taken with him and Hutch played to the gallery, promoting his Corinthians Boxing Club as his celebrity grew.

Among the famous faces photographed in his stretched hummer was boxer Mike Tyson, who hired him personally when he came to Dublin to launch his boxing pal Joe Egan's biography; The Toughest White Man On The Planet. Egan was also a close friend of Hutch. In 2006 The Monk firmly crossed the line from criminal to 'legitimate' personality when he was voted by Social and Personal magazine as one of 'Ireland's Sexiest Men.' At a glittering ceremony to mark the list he was surrounded by a bevy of beauties. In his only ever interview on television he told RTE's Prime Time that he denied any criminal activity since his 1983 prison sentence. He admitted tax evasion, but said he had made his money from shrewd property deals. The interview was filmed at the Corinthians Club where The Monk had become a coach. His main point in talking to the media was to hammer home one thing – his insistence that he wasn't involved in drugs.

Most people who knew The Monk knew that the reason for his staunch anti-drugs stance wasn't solely honourable. It would be fair to say that the north inner-city hadn't really come on all that much over the decades since the Bugsy Malones ran riot. Despite all the funding into community projects the neighbourhood had remained largely uneducated, unemployed and reliant on state handouts, which had made for a thriving black economy that was the stock and trade of the Provisional IRA. Alignment with the Provos was the golden ticket to success for any criminal, as they were the masters of many things, including money laundering, and had trusted supply lines for weapons. They also claimed to be staunchly anti-drugs and had infiltrated the Concerned Parents movements of the 1980s to cement their role in society as a paramilitary police force within communities.

The Monk had moved out of his neighbourhood, but

throughout his career he had held a 'Godfather' role within it, solving problems, making deals and creating employment – albeit the illegal kind. The people of the north inner-city were what he referred to as 'salt of the earth', they had nothing, but The Monk was confident that he had their loyalty. He knew most of them by name, particularly the women who wheeled their buggies up town and sold contraband cigarettes on street corners. Illegal fags were exactly the type of criminal enterprise that Hutch liked. As far as he was concerned nobody was getting hurt except big tobacco, it was providing work for the street traders and the customers were getting a cheap smoke. Hutch had skin in that game, although his old pal Noel Duggan was the hands-on partner. Duggan's role took him right into the dark heart of the IRA and its off-shoots and he had close links to the likes of Liam Campbell, Michael McKevitt and Colm Murphy – the Real IRA's top command who had all been found liable for bombing Omagh, an atrocity which killed 29 people, during a civil trial.

The illegal cigarette trade was a well-oiled machine that moved millions of euro of contraband from Indonesia and Thailand back to the streets of Dublin and north to the flea markets, like the one in Jonesborough in County Armagh where packets of fags sold for half the retail price. The smugglers could well afford to lose a load. They were shipping stock in 40 foot containers for an investment of less than €100,000. On the streets each shipment fetched almost €1 million.

Hutch knew the street traders by name and Duggan treated them every year to a Christmas night out and joked that each one of them could drink him under the table and even though he was paying for the evening, many had smuggled small bottles of vodka in their handbags to top up the pub measures of their favourite tipple. Old habits die hard.

A few years after his claims that he had to work for a living as a cab driver, Hutch was done having fun and settled down to enjoy life in Lanzarote, where he had purchased a beautiful villa. There, he liked to enjoy days out on luxury yachts on the Atlantic and entertain guests from back home. The weekend of his 50th birthday celebration in 2012 was a huge affair, with family and friends enjoying an all-expenses paid holiday from Dublin. Journalists from the *Sunday World* had tried to mingle nearby and pretend they were regular holidaymakers as they spied on the guests. But The Monk reckoned he was cleverer than the average fox and spotted them, keeping away from their cameras in a game of cat and mouse which only came to an end when he was carried, drunk, into a waiting taxi in the early hours of the morning. If nothing else, the picture by journalist Mick McCaffrey's team proved he was no 'Monk'. He'd hardly been home since moving out, spending more and more time on the island. But that was before all the trouble started in Spain.

*****

Unlike The Monk, Christy Kinahan Snr had never had to worry about where his next meal was coming from. He was an unusual member of gangland's fraternity, in that he had not been born into either crime or poverty. Instead he had arrived in 1957, six years before The Monk, into the bosom of a respected middle-class family who lived in Cabra, a wealthy suburb of Dublin, where period red-brick properties lined residential streets, well serviced by schools, public transport and a variety of successful businesses.

Christy was the only boy and was doted on by his sisters Denise, Maria and Sally Anne. His mother ran a B&B from the family's generous Edwardian house and their father worked as a taxi driver on a busy city centre rank. Smart and good looking, Christy was the kind of child who could have been anything, he even excelled in sports including kickboxing. But many said he was different to other kids, that he lacked empathy even at a very young age, and used his intelligence to get whatever he wanted.

Kinahan reached his 20s before he came to the attention of the gardai. At that point he had got mixed up with a gang of 'strokers', including The Monk's older brother, Eddie, known affectionately as 'Neddie', who robbed delivery vans, trucks and warehouses. While Christy wasn't much good at the hands-on work, his middle-class accent and dress sense made him useful with cashing stolen cheques or posing as a salesman to unsuspecting business people. He racked up a handful of convictions for burglary, stolen goods and using forged cheques. Kinahan had tried to settle down with Dublin beauty Jean Boylan in her local authority flat, but he was ambitious on a totally different level to her and their backgrounds were too different – despite his attempts to join working-class society. They split when their boys were only young.

While Hutch admired Martin 'The General' Cahill, whose career had seen him twice rob priceless paintings from Russborough House in County Wicklow, Kinahan was more impressed by 'Flash' Larry Dunne. Dunne, an unlikely entrepreneur and role model, had struck gold in the late 1970s when he purchased a large consignment of heroin which was selling at rock-bottom prices in Europe. Political events in Iran had sent rich Persians to the banks en masse to take what cash they could before fleeing the country. But they weren't allowed to take the money, so they had exchanged it for heroin, reselling the drug when they arrived in Europe and flooding the continent in the process.

Dunne had started to sell his 'smack' in St Teresa's Gardens, a local authority complex ravaged by unemployment and a sense of hopelessness. Heroin, which offered the ultimate escape from the realities of life, was embraced by the young, who quickly became addicted. The same happened in other local authority complexes including Dolphin House and Fatima Mansions. Dunne grew rich fast, enjoying a meteoric rise to criminal superstardom. By 1982 he was living in a mansion, had a chauffeur to drive him around and always had pretty women on his arm. Kinahan was impressed, but standing on the sidelines he was critical of Dunne and reckoned he hadn't gone near to seeing the full potential from his business. Kinahan knew he could do better and began to work away in the background on his own little empire, renting an apartment and starting to expand his contacts in the criminal world, believing that to make it rich he had to get out of sales quickly and move instead into wholesale supply.

He started to nurture contacts who had European links and eventually got an introduction to connections in the Netherlands and to the drug supermarket of Amsterdam. Kinahan was very serious about his fledgling business and to better his chances of success he set about learning Dutch, French, Arabic and studied financial tomes involving diverse business types around the world. Dunne was hated in Dublin and when he was handed a 14-year sentence in 1985 at the Central Criminal Court there were scenes of jubilation, but nobody was cheering louder than Kinahan, who saw a golden opportunity to become the biggest drug dealer to ever come out of Ireland. He was confident that what he lacked in hands-on experience he made up for with his head for business. He knew one thing from his brief career in the underworld, that his middle class accent and manners worked to his advantage and there was no reason why he couldn't make that work abroad. His ability to talk his way around anyone helped too, and as he networked with European dealers and offered them business opportunities and partnerships, he realised he was on the brink of something big.

Kinahan's plan was simple. He wanted to establish a route and a network back home, but quickly move out of Ireland and out of reach of the gardai who were starting to get tough on drug dealers. He also wagered that the quicker he moved into management the less his chances of ever getting nabbed. He worked hard and within a year of the collapse of Larry Dunne's business, Kinahan had become the main player in heroin trafficking in Ireland.

But he hadn't got out quick enough and his links with an Algerian drug dealer led the garda's drug squad to his door. When they swooped on his luxury apartment they discovered it was the hub of his operation and uncovered heroin valued at £117,000 there. In 1987, as he turned 30, he was brought before the courts charged with selling heroin. For the first time of many, he worked the system and told the court he was a heroin addict desperate to turn his life around and promised to study in prison if he was given a light sentence. He was led off to jail with a lenient six-year term and with a court order to receive a free education courtesy of the Irish taxpayer. True to his word, in prison he studied languages and took a degree in science but, vital for his future plans, he used it as a school of life and it was there that he met up with a like-minded man who would go on to become his partner in a €500 million drug empire.

John Cunningham from Ballyfermot was a wily criminal with a serious calibre. He had begun featuring in garda intelligence reports from the mid-1970s due to his involvement in armed robberies. He was a regular member of the Cahill mob and was often involved in raids of post offices. When he was part of a gang that robbed O'Connor's jewellers in Dublin and got away with a heist valued at more than €2 million, he earned his gangland stripes.

Cunningham was known for his military precision in everything he turned his hand to, a trait which earned him the nickname 'The Colonel.' Ballyfermot had spawned many major league criminals, including Gilligan and 'The Penguin' Mitchell. Like most lured to crime, Cunningham loved to live the high life and he dined and partied in top restaurants, pubs and clubs. He enjoyed holidays to Barbados and Florida but he dreamed of more than stealing for a living and always wanted 'the big one'.

When a wave of IRA kidnappings swept the country in the 1980s, Cunningham saw what he believed would be his chance to make more money than he could dream of. In 1986 he and his brother Michael decided on the family of John Guinness, who was the millionaire chairman of the Guinness Mahon bank. For eight days they held his wife Jennifer Guinness as they demanded £2 million from her wealthy husband for her safe return. But gardai rescued her from a house at Waterloo Road near the city centre following an all-night siege. The Cunninghams were arrested and sentenced to 17 years behind bars, making The Colonel and The Dapper neighbours.

In jail the pair hit it off immediately and as they mixed together during down time and over meals, they soon realised that they had more in common than their boarding facility. They shared a vision to make a major play at becoming the number one drug and weapons wholesalers into Ireland. Once up and running they believed they could offer a money laundering facility which would give them extra money to invest in their own business. They both wanted to relocate to the continent, where they believed they could become serious players on the international scene, and offer a sort of one-stop shop to Irish buyers, where they could get from them everything they needed for their criminal operations back home.

Kinahan's time would be served quickly, especially with the guaranteed remission enjoyed by all Irish prisoners, but Cunningham's biggest problem was the length of his sentence. An early plan to make a spectacular escape along with his brother fell at the first hurdle, when John Gilligan backed out of a plan to use dynamite to blow up the jail wall. Instead, he promised the brothers that he would look after their families while they languished behind bars. At first he stuck to his end of the bargain and gave the Cunningham wives supplies, like knock-off goods for street trading, to help them feed their children. After a few months he got sick of handing out loot for free, decided he wanted payment and sent a thug up to their homes to trash them. Under his orders, his enforcer terrorised the families by barging his way into their homes and smashing up furniture, windows, doors, televisions and anything else that could be broken. The short-sighted actions of Gilligan were typical of his impulsive behaviour and they would come back to haunt him many years later when he was eventually released from prison himself.

While Cunningham remained behind bars, Kinahan was released in 1991 and immediately returned to crime, as he tried to build up cash reserves to set himself up in Europe. His sons Daniel and Christopher Jnr were becoming teenagers, and in them and their friends from the north and south inner-city he saw a future army of suppliers, logistics experts and enforcers. Once he had enough money he wanted to head to Europe and leave them behind to keep his Dublin trading turf.

In the years that Kinahan had been locked up, Dublin had become increasingly violent and the garda's war on paramilitaries had firmly shifted to a war on drugs, fuelled by the vast profits being made by gangs across the city. Cocaine and cannabis were selling like never before and there were many trying to join the gold rush. Two years after he was released, Kinahan's plans were dealt another blow when he was arrested in possession of more than £16,000 worth of traveller's cheques which had been stolen in a bank robbery. He would later accuse a drug addict called Raymond Sallinger of tipping off the police. Marked as a tout, Sallinger moved to London in a sign of how dangerous the gangland outsider had become. Out on bail, Kinahan decided that he didn't want to spend another stint in prison and moved to the Netherlands, where he finally began building his dream. There, he made contact with Curtis 'Cocky' Warren, the Liverpudlian drug baron who had forged direct links with Columbian cartels, Turkish heroin suppliers and just about everyone else that Kinahan needed to know.

In September 1996, John Cunningham, transferred to Shelton Abbey open prison in Wicklow after serving 10 of his 17-year sentence, decided he was done with jail and used the prison's lax regime to simply walk out the front gates and slip out of Ireland.

In Amsterdam he hooked up with Kinahan and, in an extraordinary stroke of luck, they were in prime position there when John Gilligan's drug outfit was put out of business. At the same time, Warren had been spectacularly caught up in a major sting by Dutch police and was facing a hefty stint in jail.

In 1997, a year after Gilligan's demise, the Garda National Drug Unit seized more than 300 kilos of hash in a raid on a house in Tallaght and discovered that the drugs had been shipped into Ireland in the guise of potted plants. With a street value of more than €5 million, the seizure was significant, all the more so because it had been shipped in by Kinahan and Cunningham. It was a mark of what was to come. Not long after Cunningham's escape, Kinahan was arrested by Dutch police while in possession of ecstasy, cocaine and firearms. Jailed for four years, he again used his time to make extensive drug and gun dealing contacts and the move into the weapons market elevated him to a whole new level.

Between the Kinahan and Cunningham outfit, and George 'The Penguin' Mitchell and his business partner Tommy Savage, the Dubliners shared out the wholesale market left behind by Gilligan and much more besides. Kinahan was a quick learner and he watched as Warren landed 12 years in the tough maximum security prison in Vught for a haul of drugs, guns and cash that had been seized after his property in the Netherlands had been raided. While he wasn't out of business, Warren was weakened and Kinahan started to see the potential for muscling in. When Kinahan's father died in 1998 he made the mistake of returning for the funeral and was lifted on foot of the outstanding 1993 arrest warrant, relating to the stolen cheques. He pleaded guilty and was jailed for four years and sent to Portlaoise Prison. Sticking to the pattern, he used his time to build on his education, while Cunningham took control of the business. From prison, Kinahan was able to organise his business on a contraband mobile phone and ordered supplies for his sons and their Dublin pals. But he still had a lot to learn.

At the same time, gardai in Ireland made one of the largest ever weapon and drug seizures, when they discovered 800 kilos of cannabis, 15 machine guns, 10 pistols and a large amount of ammunition in a cold store at Castleblayney in County Monaghan. The weapons had been manufactured in Eastern Europe.

They set about tracing the load and discovered the shipment had come from an Amsterdam coffee shop. Gardai passed the information on to their Dutch counterparts and Amsterdam's Serious Crime Squad began to watch the premises. They sent the pictures back to Dublin and the familiar face of John Cunningham was identified meeting with the owner. While he was a fugitive from Ireland, it was agreed that undercover officers would start to watch him and establish exactly how he was doing business.

For four months they listened into his phones and watched him. The firearms, they discovered, were coming from Joopie Alteposts, an Eastern European contact of Kinahan from jail in the Netherlands. They also learned that Cunningham and his associates were manufacturing their own ecstasy by sourcing powder in Holland and using a network of flats equipped with tablet-making machines. Each tablet was costing £1 to make and was then being sold on for £4, a massive profit which was then being laundered through Kinahan's expertise and contacts.

Cannabis and cocaine were also being sourced in Amsterdam and officers watched while Cunningham prepared the shipments, often hiding the drugs and firearms in pallets of foodstuff. The tap on the phones identified their key customers in Ireland, Northern Ireland, Belgium and even France. In March 2000, Cunningham was spectacularly nabbed as he loaded a van packed with flowers, a tonne of cannabis and 100,000 ecstasy pills. Under the blocks of cannabis were three machine guns – and Cunningham was carrying a loaded pistol.

In his home at Weteringbrug, outside Amsterdam, follow-up searches netted drugs, handguns and ammunition. A van met earlier by him was stopped and 1,000 kilos of cannabis and 30 kilos of ecstasy, worth more than €15 million, were discovered.

Back in Ireland, gardai searched 13 addresses across Dublin and arrested seven. Five were later charged with drug trafficking and money laundering offences and sentenced to 18 years between them. A ledger was discovered which revealed that in one four-month period Cunningham had shipped hash and ecstasy with a street value of €31 million to Dublin. The Irish end of the business was estimated to be worth €100 million. In Portlaoise Prison, Kinahan was livid. He lashed out looking for a scapegoat and blamed The General's old sidekick, Martin 'The Viper' Foley, who found himself staring down the barrel of a gun within months of the bust, surviving his third shooting.

Cunningham remained in custody in the Netherlands as he awaited trial and just after it began, the haulier Kieran Smyth was found dead in a field in County Meath. He had been bound and gagged and shot through the head at close range, his body dumped in a cattle pen. Cunningham was found guilty on drug charges and handed down a nine-year sentence, hefty by Dutch standards, but also meaning he'd be returned to Ireland for another six years for his role in the Guinness kidnapping. It seemed his past had finally caught up with him.

But one month after Cunningham's conviction, Christy Kinahan was released from jail where he moved straight to the UK, and it all started again. There, he married a Dutch woman and settled down in North Surrey, registering a number of businesses including tanning and beauty shops as well as car dealerships and construction firms. The pair shared a house in Chertsey where Daniel and brother Christopher Jnr were later registered as residents. But Kinahan was soon on the move, travelling around Europe and particularly between the Netherlands and Spain. He had an empire to build as an eager army came of age.

Back in Dublin the next generation of keen young criminals were about to find themselves perfectly positioned as the new foot soldiers for the emerging Irish mafia. The Monk's world of cunning robberies and spoil-sharing with the Provos was becoming a thing of the past and, despite his shaky start in gangland, it seemed that Kinahan was looking like the one to bet on. In Oliver Bond in the south inner-city the Kinahan boys had created their own brat pack and were flogging their father's supplies of ecstasy and cocaine to a hungry market.

South to Crumlin, a violent gang of John Gilligan's young protégés were eager to hop aboard. North into the inner-city and further up towards Hardwicke Street flats a new breed of criminal, many of whom came from families once active in the Concerned Parents Against Drugs group, were ready, too, for success. And then there was the next generation of Hutch, led by the fast-living Gary. A joyrider, drug dealer and violent criminal, he had made a decision early in life that he wasn't going to wait until his 50s to enjoy the fruits of his labour. He may have been Hutch by name but he was going to prove that he was much more Kinahan by nature.

3

The Brat Pack

There were no early signs that Daniel Kinahan had what it would take to run a mob, but by the time of the murder of Gary Hutch he was surrounded by dangerous, ruthless and loyal soldiers who had been plucked from the four corners of Dublin.

Growing up in Oliver Bond in the south inner-city, the Kinahan boys could have gone unnoticed had they not had the reputation of their father to lean on. The Bond, as it was affectionately known, was a large local authority flat complex sitting beside the giant Guinness Factory, which emitted its pungent aroma of hops into the air like a massive set of bag-pipes.

The original Guinness family were a hugely wealthy Anglo-Irish protestant clan who made millions through brewing, banking and politics. But when Arthur Guinness took out a 9,000-year lease on four acres at St James's Gate in Dublin, signed on December 31st 1759, he would cement the family name in history for centuries to come. By the late 1800s Arthur was gone but his offspring took over the family brewery and began a series of charitable initiatives to better the lives of their workers. They introduced free medical care and meals, as well as building homes for their staff to rent which culminated in the establishment of the Iveagh Trust in 1890, created to provide housing for the poor.

Amongst its projects was the Iveagh Markets, a vast indoor structure to allow the poor to trade their wares in shelter and warmth and where generations of south inner-city families sold vegetables, fruit, fish and even rags to keep the wolves from their doors. Oliver Bond was built in blocks named A to T in the 1930s by the newly-formed Irish State to provide housing for those who got jobs at Guinness and in the bustling textile factories nearby where clothing, shoes and uniforms were made. When most of the industry disappeared in the 1970s and 1980s, it was never replaced and instead of factory jobs, the dole queues beckoned the young, while the old tried to flog their wares in the increasingly run-down Iveagh Market. By the turn of the century the market was closed, its bustling halls a thing of the past, but promises of rejuvenation bought votes and Dublin was about to sell its soul to developers and multi-nationals feeding an ever greater rift between rich and poor.

In 1999, on the day of the announcement of a £15 million refurbishment project for the Iveagh Markets the then Taoiseach Bertie Ahern made an official visit to St Nicholas and Myra Parish Hall. The *Irish Times* was there to record the occasion and detail how the women traders had dressed in black outfits and aprons to serve trays of sandwiches and canapés to the gathered crowd.

In a small article the paper reported how during the ceremony a grandmother pushed forward a 'shy' Daniel Kinahan and joked: "Give him a plug," telling the journalist that he had just started to work as a furniture restorer. At that time, Kinahan, born June 25th, 1977, was listed as a director of four different companies, namely Coombes. K Furniture Specialists, Fairfold Limited, The Curious Cat and Green Clean Clinical Limited – all of which would be dissolved within a few years. Just months earlier Kinahan had made his first front-page appearance in the *Sunday World* – but it wasn't for his carpentry skills. Under the headline 'The Brat Pack' and with his face blurred due to legal restrictions, the tabloid newspaper known for its edgy crime coverage had listed him at the top of a crew of young dealers who were making their name in the capital's lucrative drug supply market. Kinahan had been arrested when he and a group of friends clashed with an off-duty garda outside a Dublin dog track. He was amongst those prosecuted, although the charges against him were later dropped. Outside the Four Courts he cut a swagger that wasn't 'licked off the ground'. It was a confidence that came from the status of his birth.

Unlike many of the street thugs who vied for supremacy in the brutal drugs underworld, the Kinahan brothers never had to prove their brawn to become top dogs on their own home turf. With their father and Cunningham firmly positioned as European wholesalers by the 1990s, albeit as they meandered in and out of prison, the brothers took on a supplier role in Dublin which gave them a popularity amongst groups across the city and cemented their own position in the food chain.

Daniel was particularly ambitious on two fronts. Firstly, he wanted the wealth and lifestyle of his father and, secondly, he wanted to prove to him that he was a chip off the old block and every bit as ruthless. Christopher Jnr, or 'Git', on the other hand was socially awkward and preferred to remain in the background. He believed he had a head for business, like his father.

The brothers' circle of childhood friends knew the Kinahan boys were their best chance of making it to the big league and so they stayed close, many allowing Daniel to assume the role of a gang boss. He revelled in his popularity and often played the clown. Hopping out of cars to apprehend drug users while pretending to be a garda was one of his party pieces and when he did, everyone would laugh. "Danny was loud, he always had to be noticed no matter where we were," a former pal would tell me in recent years. "He liked to be the centre of attention and to be right. He was always right, even when he was wrong. You knew just to go along with him because there was a menace to him and it was just easier when he saw you as being on his side. He did have quite a dynamic personality and he was great fun to be with. There was always a game with him, especially when it came to women. If you were out with him, even just on a shopping trip, he'd get all these phone numbers from random girls. He'd just tell you he'd be back in a minute and the next thing we'd see him chatting up some good-looking bird. He always came back with their phone number, which of course was funny. He was a charmer and he was good looking and he knew how to get what he wanted from people. He was with all the girls and he had his pick of them. He'd no loyalty to anyone in particular but he made them all feel special at the same time. Git was totally different. He had a job in the council where he could get bits of information but he was quieter and seemed to just go along with Danny. Danny was definitely the boss."

Friends were a small tight circle and were loyal to the core, following 'Danny' around and doing his bidding. Some were slower to warm to his charms, including James Quinn who was dating a relative of the brothers. A nephew of the well-known criminal Martin 'The Viper' Foley, Quinn was a good boxer and often fought in illegal bare knuckle battles where he would more often than not lay his opponents out in the early rounds. Davin Flynn, who was older than the brothers, helped them network and saw the potential of friendship with them. Oliver Bond was full of drugs and it was perfectly designed for privacy and a quick escape.

Dealers openly sold heroin in the courtyards and around the stairwells to users who would wander in from the city streets outside through an archway which was the only way in and out. It seemed like the majority were at the very least smoking joints like cigarettes. "That's what was different about Danny. He never used," his pal told me. "He would often have bits of cannabis but he would ask the guys to smoke it and tell him what they thought of it. He'd be wondering what the quality of it was like. He was a fit lad and he didn't seem to drink either. He was into women, he liked to eat out but he was always in control. Back then Danny was very anti-heroin, or so he said. Well, his ma did bits with the community workers who looked after the addicts so he only ever had cannabis."

Smack dealing in the flats was left to Greg Lynch and he ran The Bond like clockwork with a supply sourced from his uncle, Gerard 'Hatchet' Kavanagh, an associate of the Dapper Don. Lynch was known as an oddball but respected the Kinahans' place in his patch and while he wasn't close with either of the brothers they afforded each other a reverence. As unemployment had skyrocketed through the 1980s and into the 1990s in local authority areas, business boomed for the drug industry and not only in the inner-city but also south to Crumlin, where the value of cocaine territory was about to be felt like never before. There, the Kinahan brothers and their crew from The Bond would find allies who possessed a ruthlessness the likes of which had never been seen before.

From an early age Freddie Thompson was the one to watch around the Liberties and in the turf west on the canals and away from the city. As a teenager he excelled at two things – coming to the attention of gardai and his ability to handle himself in the boxing ring. At his local club, he was a quick and powerful fighter who stood out as a fearless opponent, never afraid to hurt or injure anyone he was pitted against. Thompson had stopped growing by the time he was around 13 and at 5 foot 8 inches he was hardly an impressive height. However, he made up for his lack of stature with his ability to give savage beatings for little or no reason and in particular for any perceived slight. He showed a coldness that was reflected in his steely eyes which rarely changed expression. Some people noted that even when Freddie smiled, his eyes did not.

His cousins were the Byrne brothers, David and Liam, who had a reputation for being violent bullies in their hometown of Crumlin, just a few kilometres west of the Liberties. Crumlin had long been a hotbed of crime and was home to the early godfathers, many of whom had become rich and famous on their own reputations and ability to outsmart the police. Freddie was hooked on the whiff of sulphur that hung in the air in Crumlin and he idolised the likes of Martin 'The General' Cahill and his sidekicks 'The Viper', Seamus 'Shavo' Hogan and Jimmy 'The Whale' Gantley and the tales of their daring robberies and extortions that had made them famous.

By 1994 when Cahill was murdered in Ranelagh, 14-year-old Freddie was already on the fringes of a large, young and rapidly forming drug gang who were working for John Gilligan and his partners, north inner-city hood Peter 'Fatso' Mitchell and John 'The Coach' Traynor, who had established themselves as suppliers of cannabis. Two of Freddie's superiors, Brian Rattigan and Declan Gavin, were perfect in Gilligan's eyes. He needed to shift his product and they were young hungry dealers. Despite being only teenagers they were heavily involved in his supply chain and made regular trips to Amsterdam and Spain. Gilligan had even trusted them to meet some of the suppliers that he used.

Gilligan's immense personal wealth and his lack of restraint in showing it off is what had led him to become a person of interest for the crime journalist Veronica Guerin. When Gilligan ordered the journalist's murder in June 1996, which was carried out by members of his gang, his ill-conceived plan to silence her backfired spectacularly and his business was shut down almost overnight by a massive garda crackdown.

The demise of Gilligan had left a huge vacuum to be filled by anyone in the right place and at the right time and Rattigan and Gavin grabbed the opportunity with both hands, using the skills and the contacts the drug boss had given them. Everyone moved up a notch and that meant Freddie Thompson, too. Quickly, he started to morph from street dealer to large supplier as he turned hundreds of euro into thousands and began to wholesale to some of the toughest estates and flat complexes in Dublin. His ruthless approach to business coupled with his boxing skills and connections made him a feared figure in an already tough underworld.

Years after he'd terrorised his way to a position of power and had secured a seat at the Dapper Don's top table, I'd met one of his dealers. He was a boxer too, six foot tall and with a madness that had drawn him right into the heart of the underworld. He spoke of slicing up 'junkies' and beating prostitutes who tried to rip him off. He wasn't a coward, and I gathered he'd have been far more comfortable taking on someone of his own size and strength, but he was afraid of Freddie Thompson and I could see it in his eyes years later. That was why he had done those things which would haunt him until the day he died. Facing his maker with his soul laid bare and his sins in his two hands was a far easier concept than telling Thompson he'd been ripped off.

Under Freddie's rules, street dealers could earn up to €500 a day clear profit and up to €1,500 depending on how hard they worked. The longer they sold, the more customers they could catch. He got a cut from every sale and in order to make sure that nobody moved in on his territory he ran a tight ship where there was no tick allowed. To hammer home his power to the population of hopeless addicts queuing up for his wares, he often ordered a horrific beating or stabbing as a reminder of who was boss. Regularly, he would do the job himself and appeared to get a kick out of inflicting pain and injury on the helpless.

Thompson was an addict too – to the profits that could be made from buying and selling drugs, to the lifestyle, but more so to the overwhelming sense of power he felt every time he walked down a street and saw someone look at him in fear. His reputation was such that he had forged links with the northside and right into Hutch territory, where he had developed a close friendship with Paddy Doyle, a notoriously violent childhood friend of Gary Hutch.

Thompson idolised Gavin but never got on so well with Rattigan and for years the gang just about held things together as their new order settled in, but in the drugs world there is never room for two. Gavin and Rattigan were two alpha males and they were young and volatile. Assaults, criminal damage and tit-for-tat violence soon began to intensify into a feud.

In 2000 a seizure of €1.7 million of cocaine and ecstasy in the Holiday Inn Hotel on Dublin's Pearse Street changed everything. Gavin along with two pals, Graham 'The Wig' Whelan and Philip Griffiths, worked through the night to break up the large block of cocaine into individual one-gram deals which they could sell for €80 a bag. Breaking, grinding, mixing and weighing the coke was about the hardest work they would have to do for their share of €750,000 profit on the consignment, which was due to be divided between about 10 teenage drug dealers including Brian Rattigan.

When cops burst in, Whelan and Griffiths were literally caught red-handed with the drugs, but Gavin was having a lie down and wasn't physically touching any of the gear, meaning he had to be released after questioning. While many may see that as a stroke of luck, in the paranoid drugs underworld there are no coincidences and good fortune only exists for those who make their own. Rattigan immediately pointed the finger at his business partner, accusing him of being a garda informant.

Gavin levelled the same accusations at Rattigan, and in the days and weeks that followed the Crumlin and Drimnagh gang drew battle lines – clearly divided for ever more.

Firmly by Gavin's side was Freddie Thompson, his friend Paddy Doyle and money man Darren Geoghegan. Doyle was not the brightest, but what he lacked in smarts he made up for in muscle and in coldness and he was, in the minds of many who encountered him, a natural born killer. Geoghegan was very bright and able to manage the money laundering, while Thompson was violent, ruthless and had sociopathic tendencies with a good dose of narcissism thrown in.

A year after the Holiday Inn bust, Brian Rattigan was celebrating his little brother Joey's 18th birthday when, full of cocaine, he heard Gavin was in the local Abrakebabra ordering a takeaway. Rattigan was red eyed and sniffing frantically when he got out of the screeching Nissan Micra, lifted his balaclava and showed Gavin the large knife he had brought with him. "Do you remember me?" he said, before launching himself at Gavin and stabbing him repeatedly. It would be the first murder of 16 in what became known as the Crumlin Drimnagh feud. In a matter of hours, Freddie Thompson had stepped forward and taken the reins from the murdered Gavin and in the years that followed, under his authority, his gang would murder the way most people order a pizza.

Amongst his victims would be Rattigan's beloved little brother, Joey. During his 10-year murder spree Thompson was backed by his cousins, the Byrne brothers, who had gone from schoolyard bullies to major league criminals, in no time thanks to their lineage. Not only was their father a master forger who had often worked with Christy Kinahan Snr but their sister, Joanne, had married one of the most feared gangsters in modern criminal history. Thomas 'Bomber' Kavanagh had been on the garda radar for decades and was known as a ruthless drug boss who studied the science of fear. 'Bomber' had made a lot of money out of crime and when the CAB had been set up he was one of the first targets of it. In 1998 he was named along with George 'The Penguin' Mitchell when the Bureau got High Court judgements against them. In court, Kavanagh claimed that his modest home on Knocknarea Road in Drimnagh was his only asset and he eventually had to hand it over.

In the years after the proceedings he and Joanne had moved to Birmingham. There, he had teamed up with two drug-dealing cousins, James Mulvey in Solihull and Gerard 'Hatchet' Kavanagh, back in Dublin. Together, they became key suppliers of product into Ireland and the UK, with Kinahan drugs and weapons. After 'Bomber' settled in the UK, 'Hatchet' moved out to the Costa, to Benalmadena, leaving his younger brother Paul and nephew Greg Lynch at home to look after his interests.

At Hardwicke Street flats, north of the city centre and a notorious drug hotspot, another young mob had emerged. Despite the large local authority complex being the birthplace of Concerned Parents Against Drugs (CPAD), the younger breed knew there was just one sure way to get rich. The likes of Ross Browning trod a well-worn path into the world of gangs, criminality and the company of the Kinahan brothers and their cohorts. CPAD, which had marched on the homes of drug dealers and forced suppliers out of the area, had once been feared and revered under its founding member

John 'Whacker' Humphries, but those days were gone. When his parents split up Ross lived with his mum Julie Conway, a cleaner, who was surrounded by a large extended family within the north inner-city area. His father Kieran was an absentee parent and instead Browning befriended the older Gary Finnegan and found a mentor to draw him into crime as a means to make a living. As a teenager he was caught carrying out the robbery of a Securicor van along with Barry Finnegan, Gary's younger cousin, and their childhood pal Robert Browne. As the millennium dawned Ross was 20, unemployed, but with a penchant for fast cars and connections with ambitious drug dealers. A fitness fanatic who loved to box, he was also handy with his fists, making him a perfect enforcer and debt collector.

Nearby, in Hutch territory, Gary Hutch, his brother Derek 'Del Boy' and their large circle of associates were never going to be left behind. While the older generation and particularly family godfather The Monk cared about their image, the offspring were not so prudish and made no secret of their involvement in the drugs trade. Gary idolised The Monk but he shared none of his qualities. The Monk was a controlled, thoughtful criminal, while Gary's formative years were poisoned by the drug culture around him. While he had formed his own band of brothers, just like his uncle, his were a chaotic bunch who lived on a diet of cocaine, ecstasy and violence. He'd started out as a young joyrider who loved being behind the wheel of a fast car and had made quite a living out of his skills. He had a madness about him but could also keep his nerve on a job.

At the turn of the millennium, Hutch was before the courts on his first serious charge. It was connected to his role in the robbery of jewellery and cash from a house in Malahide in Dublin, during which a businessman and his wife had been put through a terrifying ordeal. The €40,000 worth of jewellery and €8,000 wouldn't have been a bad day's work had they got away with it, but they were caught and Hutch was jailed for six years. But history has a habit of repeating itself and in prison he soon had a Road to Damascus moment, when he realised that house burglary was too high risk and not for him and he'd confine himself to big cash jobs in future, where there would be a higher profit margin. More importantly, he'd vowed that he would invest his proceeds wisely, directly into drugs, to increase his margins.

At the same time that the young bloods were coming of age, the Irish economy began to boom and construction took off like never before. Hundreds of thousands of labourers, tradesmen and builders found themselves rich beyond their wildest dreams and as the money flowed in, it flooded straight back out again and into the hands of the cannabis and cocaine dealers, who were finding the demand for their product at an all-time high.

The UK and Europe were already embracing their love affair with coke, ecstasy and cannabis. Despite Cunningham's incarceration, Kinahan was riding a wave of success from Amsterdam along with a tight team of armed robbers, enforcers and money launderers he had recruited in his time behind bars. Together they were starting to move vast amounts of ecstasy, sourced in Holland, cannabis and cocaine into the UK and Ireland. Kinahan was mixing with all the right people to ensure he kept on top of his business.

Amongst them was Mink Kok, a notorious Dutch drug and

arms dealer who had quit law school to join a Kubbutz in Israel. There, he had learned Hebrew and used it to enhance his ecstasy trade and connections in Lebanon's hash markets. Kinahan Snr was impressed by Kok's manner and his business prowess in offering a one-stop shop for all the tools of gangland crime. Kinahan learned a lot from the more sophisticated European crooks and was skilled in replicating their money laundering ideas, developing a slick network of businesses with which to wash his dirty money.

But Kinahan needed a presence in Spain too on the Costa Del Sol, where cannabis sourced from Morocco was landed in boats along the coastline and deals could be made with cocaine traders from Central and South America. He had the contacts but needed a trusted associate based there to look after his interests and deal directly with suppliers from Tangier. While Daniel was desperate for a role on the international side of his father's business, the Dapper Don felt his son was lacking experience and sent his own protégé to Marbella to set up a base instead.

Although the same age as his eldest son, Kinahan's chosen lieutenant called 'Sam' had a background more similar to the Dapper Don than his own offspring. Reared in an affluent south county Dublin home, Sam spoke nothing like the rough Dubliners which the Kinahan boys were surrounded with. He had met up with Kinahan Snr while selling ecstasy in clubs in Dublin and had quickly proved his worth as a trusted member of his inner circle. Cold and dedicated to the tough world of international organised crime, he had shown his loyalty, his icy approach to deals and his ability to soak up every aspect of the business of drugs and weapons dealing. More importantly, he had been able to leave Dublin behind and focus totally on the importance of becoming a slick-talking European. 'Sam' wasn't long in Spain before he had made some vital contacts for his boss. They included young English criminals who were close with some of the elders who had been running the lucrative Costa Del Crime for decades and who had long-term associations into the heart of North Africa and with the cocaine cowboys who represented their cartels on the coast.

Kinahan's rise wasn't going unnoticed by police forces. Two years after his release from Portlaoise Prison, the Garda National Drugs Unit launched Operation Zombie to target Kinahan and his inner circle. They consulted with their counterparts in Spain, Holland, Belgium and the UK where the gang's drugs and guns were being sourced, moved and sold. Intelligence suggested that Kinahan often travelled alongside his supply, but always remained hands-off and at a distance as he oversaw the operations.

In the UK, major seizures of cannabis hidden in tiles from Alicante and in other shipments had been linked to him and concerns were growing that he was becoming a significant player in Scotland, too, with links to a Glasgow gang headed up by Stephen Lyons. Each route busted suggested that millions of euros worth of drugs had already got through.

In Ireland, Kinahan had made connections with feuding Limerick mobs and begun supplying them with drugs and weapons smuggled through a large network of food supplies and any exportable product. Gardai, like their counterparts in Europe, were facing major policing challenges and their 2002 report highlighted particular areas, like the expansion of the European Union, the removal of border controls throughout the EU and increased global trade as examples of problems facing investigators. Other criminals who were benefiting from open trade included George 'The Penguin' Mitchell, who had established himself in the Netherlands and who had moved his entire family out to Amsterdam to join him. There, in 2000, his son-in-law, Derek 'Maradona' Dunne, had been shot dead – but business continued for Mitchell.

Also a player on the international scene at that time was the other Mitchell, aka Peter 'Fatso', who had slipped the net of the Veronica Guerin murder team and had established himself between Puerto Banus and Amsterdam, with partners from Liverpool. He often worked with The Penguin and was in regular contact with John 'The Coach' Traynor who was moving between the Netherlands and Margate on the UK's south coast.

Some successes were made against Kinahan. One of the biggest came when undercover officers tailed a van to the Slade Valley Equestrian Club near Rathcoole in Dublin, where 500 kilos of hash and automatic weapons were found. A street value of nearly €20 million was put on the haul, representing a loss to Kinahan of a paltry €2 million. A year later 'Operation Embargo' was launched in the UK against Kinahan. During the investigation it emerged that his mob had supplied half a tonne of cocaine to a family in London. The Adams – or the A team as they were also known – were one of the most powerful and feared crime gangs in the UK in the 1980s and 1990s and were credited with murdering legendary rival mobster 'Mad' Frankie Fraser along with 25 others. They had enjoyed close links with the Colombian Cartels but their power had waned from 2000 on, and Kinahan had become their middle man.

CLASH OF THE CLANS

As his business flourished, Kinahan remained determined to reach the very top of the European crime ladder, but he was also intent on schooling his sons in his art. The Kinahan boys began to travel between the UK, Ireland and Spain with Daniel in particular laying down roots on the Costa, where he hooked up with his father's favourite 'Sam'. On the face of it the pair got on perfectly OK with Daniel politely integrating himself into the Spanish scene where 'Sam' had recruited a group of fast-living enthusiasts who wanted to make their mark on the Costa Del Crime. While drug dealers had to be careful how they spent their money back in Ireland, where the Criminal Assets Bureau were always watching, in Spain nobody asked any questions of an unemployed twenty-something from a notorious local authority flat complex in Dublin and their ability to afford a Ferrari, penthouse apartment and regular shopping sprees at the Corte Ingles. 'Danny' was charming and always took the bill when the group met up for meals or nights out. He purchased a stunning apartment in a gated development and quickly a villa with its own pool. While 'Sam' was the one who travelled up and back to the Netherlands and Belgium to meet with the Dapper Don, 'Danny' would publicly talk to him on the phone always signing off by telling him: "I love you."

He quickly met a Dublin girl, a Costa socialite who was friendly with his aunt Denise, and she moved in with him while accompanying him to country club lunches and to posh eateries in Puerto Banus. While it would take some time to realise how significant those few years were, for the Kinahan gang what was unmistakable was they were becoming very rich, very quickly and in large part it was thanks to Warren.

46

Over his lengthy career in the drugs business, Warren had excelled in cutting out the middle men and dealing directly with the suppliers of wholesale drugs to Europe. Aside from the Colombians and the Turks, he had also forged contacts with Moroccan hash growers. He was clever and crafty and impossibly rich, netting himself an eye-watering fortune topping €200 million, which had got him listed in the *Sunday Times* rich list, before a court heard how he'd really made his money. Warren had close connections to Ireland but his big markets were the large cities of London, Liverpool, Birmingham, Manchester and Leeds – each of which could individually rival the Irish market in total. In the Netherlands he had settled down to live a life that he believed was under the radar and out of the way but he didn't realise that surveillance laws had allowed Dutch police to tap his phones in the same way they would with Cunningham years later. While he had continued to run his business from jail, Kinahan had quickly moved in on some of his customers and connections, mopping up what he could.

In Spain, 'Sam' and 'Danny' had hooked up with two of Warren's former protégés, Merseyside brothers Andy and Gary Murphy, who were on the run from drug convictions in the UK. The pair had set up a warehousing service outside Marbella to store and transport drugs back to the UK. They needed all the logistics they could get as they were landing tonnes of high-quality Tangier weed on beaches along the Costa, so much that they had to keep coming up with new and innovative ways of transporting it. Anything from jars of olives, wooden pallets and tins of tomatoes were used while the money simply flooded in, hundreds of thousands every week.

The English mobsters introduced their Irish contemporaries to the Moroccan dealers and one in particular known as 'The Fat Man', who hosted them in his mansion on exotic rugs surrounded with expensive art and entertained them in his private riad filled with antique roses and fruit trees. "I can guarantee to land the hashish," he told them. "On the beaches near Tarifa. You won't have a problem." And they never did. Each shipment arrived as planned and was transported up the coast to the Murphy warehouses in high-speed cars stripped of their seats to ensure the loads could fit. The money just kept coming.

Despite his success and wealth, Kinahan Snr never forgave or forgot. Back in Dublin in 2003, Raymond Salinger, the man blamed for the cheque forgery information, was watching a Leeds v Chelsea match in Farrell's of New Street in Dublin when two men walked in wearing balaclavas and calmly shot him dead. The men under the balaclavas were believed to be two of Daniel Kinahan's protégés but nobody was ever charged. Shortly after the murder Gary Hutch, who was a garda suspect in the assassination, landed a role in Amsterdam organising drug consignments. When the Murphy brothers were arrested and returned to the UK, new warehouses were found and the conveyor belt started all over again.

Kinahan Snr remained totally paranoid about the police. Whenever he met members of his gang he did so after arrangements worthy of scenes in spy movies. Often he would change the venue, anything up to five or six times over a morning, and always spoke in code. Some would complain how they had to eat numerous breakfasts in various hotels before the Dapper Don would actually show up. While Danny had brought in some of his childhood friends from Oliver Bond, Kinahan Snr saw 'Sam' as being more like himself as he came from a middle-class background and had more polished manners. Beneath the surface, many believed that 'Danny' grew envious of his father's relationship with the outsider and when he and three others were nabbed by Spanish police while transporting cannabis, 'Sam' couldn't help but wonder if he'd been framed. While Spanish police were often placated with a payment of a few hundred euros, the four were brought to court and found themselves in front of a judge who jailed them for two years.

With 'Sam' behind bars, Danny took a more hands-on role on the Costa. Kinahan could see his sons as they went from boys to men within the world of international crime. In Daniel he saw his own steely determination and ability to make business decisions without emotion. In Christopher Jnr he had a willing student in the art of money laundering – the key component in any drug empire.

While the Dapper Don was known for his covert behaviour, habits he tried to instil in all his young protégés, the activities of his sons didn't go unnoticed and UK police noted Daniel Kinahan's presence at a number of horse race meetings, as they investigated a race fixing scandal involving organised criminals. In May 2004 police put what they believed was a 'race to lose' syndicate under surveillance and watched as Daniel Kinahan travelled from Spain to Newmarket, where he and associates attempted to visit the jockey Kieren Fallon's home in the early hours of the morning.

Cops believed that a syndicate of gamblers had lost €231,000 just days beforehand, when Fallon had won the race on Russian

Rhythm, who hailed from the stables of Queen Elizabeth's favourite trainer, Sir Michael Stout. Officers suspected the syndicate were none too happy, as they had backed the horse to lose, and they watched as the young Kinahan and an associate travelled to Harrogate to the Bedford Lodge Hotel in Newmarket, where they checked in under false names and used cash to pay. At 1am Kinahan and two others drove out to visit Fallon at his family home, only to turn back when they realised they were under surveillance. They checked out of the hotel at 2am. While Fallon and others would later be acquitted after a major trial at the Old Bailey, a series of intercepted phone conversations heard Daniel Kinahan being described as a 'formidable' and 'menacing' character. "He is only a little fella but you know when you've been spoken to," the court heard in taped chats.

Despite the millions being turned over by the organisation, Kinahan Snr was desperate for more investment funds. He wanted to buy ever-larger consignments of drugs to lessen his transport costs and increase supply. The Kinahans were quickly gaining a reputation for being ruthless in their business methods. While in some drug organisations losses are factored into the turnover, within the Kinahan organisation they were not, and a bullet awaited anyone blamed for a slip-up. Businessman Boudewijn Kerbusch, from the Netherlands, thought he'd get rich when he was recruited to smuggle drugs into Ireland in fish and seafood shipments. But when 700 kilos of his load was nabbed by UK police in June 2004, he was shot dead. Many more would follow.

While Amsterdam, London, Birmingham, Antwerp, Rotterdam, Liverpool and Dublin were key market places,

Puerto Banus, the playboy port of the Costa Del Sol was, by the mid 2000s, firmly established as the Kinahan mob headquarters. Senior members of the organisation, including the Dapper Don, began to buy up property in the Marbella hills and in the gated complexes near Estepona's so-called 'Golden Mile'.

Cunningham, released from jail and back in his position at the top table, moved to Alicante, down the coast, a second hub for drug buying, transportation and weapons procurement. For the young Dublin dealers who were making their way up the ranks of Kinahan's empire, Spain was the ultimate finishing school and they couldn't wait to taste success.

As the mob grew and more Dubliners moved out to Spain, Cunningham became concerned. He didn't like the rough cocaine users who seemed to be flocking around the carefully built business and drawing attention to the well-honed machine that was bringing in millions on a monthly basis. But Kinahan Snr wouldn't entertain any concerns about his boys. He may not have been at their side as they grew up in The Bond, but he intended to show them that his absence as a father in years past was only so he could build a very special future for them.

Back in Dublin, by early 2005, Thompson had gained the notorious status of a terrifying gangland star known simply as 'Fat' Freddie in the tabloid media. Even the then Minister of Justice, Michael McDowell, announced an extra 15,000 garda hours to combat gun crime caused by his wave of violence. Towards the end of the year, when three men were killed within days, McDowell had to assure the public that he had control of the situation and Thompson's hitman, Paddy Doyle, became Ireland's most wanted man.

The pressure was such that within a month Doyle was gone to Spain for a new life and Thompson had fled to the Netherlands, where he hooked up with Gary Hutch. The pair were to become Kinahan Snr's 'logistics men', a trusted job to do deals for large drug consignments and transport them onwards. In Rotterdam in October 2006, Thompson was arrested following a seizure of machine guns and 7kgs of cocaine. But he had luck on his side, and the Dutch magistrate threw the case out when it came before him because he was in a lobby of the building at the time of the raid and could have been innocent. The judge even made the authorities compensate Thompson for the time he spent in jail – delighting the criminal.

Thompson returned to Dublin but soon left for Spain where he presumed he would be welcomed at the Kinahan top table. He was wrong. For some reason Daniel Kinahan had taken a turn against him and, to humiliate him, ordered him to cut his lawn. But his exile was brief as he was too useful as a killing machine to be left out in the cold for long and he had retained a strong grip on vast territories of Dublin's drug turf.

Hutch and Thompson moved back and forth between the Netherlands and Spain, but while both were immersed in the Kinahan mob they still socialised heavily with Paddy Doyle. He had gone his own way since he had washed up on the Costa, where he had joined the ranks of his old neighbour 'Fatso' Mitchell's outfit. At that point Mitchell was 10 years in Spain, seriously well connected and knew how to keep the Dapper Don on side. Doyle, however, feared no-one and scoffed at the reverence some treated Daniel with, often making fun of him behind his back.

The garda were concerned about how the Irish mobs were growing their powerbase on the Costa. But in Spain, their policing system is made up by three separate forces. They were disjointed and overwhelmed by the concentration of organised crime groups on the southern coast. The likes of the Moroccans and the Russians – who had a reputation for narco-style violence – often took priority when it came to policing crackdowns, as their presence was a threat to the all-important tourism sector.

For the gangsters, Spain was a testosterone super highway and at the Plaza Gym, near Puerto Banus, Irish and UK mobsters mixed together while pumping weights and showcasing their abs. There, Thompson cooked up a plan to pretend he was dead and laughed when newspapers in Ireland reported that he was missing without trace with a €100,000 contract on his head. As the drugs flooded home, gardai tried desperately to quell the tide, but with gangs operating with near impunity in Spain and the Netherlands it was an almost impossible task.

In the UK, Mulvey and Bomber's Birmingham-based outfit were targeted in two investigations. The first related to a consignment of industrialised metal rollers, which when searched contained 21kg blocks of 83% pure cocaine, 365kg of cannabis and 10kg of mixing agent. The drugs were trafficked from Belgium and destined for Ireland. The investigation established that 14 similar deliveries had been made to Dublin using the same method by a transportation company owned by Mulvey called JBS Transport Ltd. When the police discovered this method of drug smuggling, JBS Transport found another way. They arranged for an employee to collect and deliver drugs to Ireland using C-scooters and replica Harley Davidson motorbikes. They did it five times before they were caught. A number of people were arrested and sentenced to lengthy prison terms, but Mulvey slipped the net and went on the run, leaving Bomber to run the show.

In May 2007, the kind of connections Kinahan Snr had made and his elevated rankings in the world of international crime became apparent when he returned to Ireland for the wedding of his son, Christopher Jnr. The Dapper Don, usually careful not to show his hand back in Ireland, threw caution to the wind and splashed out on a lavish ceremony while also using the occasion as a crime summit with his main partners. It was still boom times in Ireland but when the luxurious Marriot Hotel in county Wicklow was handed an €11,000 cash deposit for a wedding due to take place on Friday September 7th, eyebrows were raised. The female who handed over the money didn't want a receipt and had no concerns about the cost of anything at the five-star venue. The booking was written into the reservations but the address of the bride and groom of Oliver Bond House and working-class Herberton Road in Rialto looked even odder. Neither came from the usual middle-class areas associated with the Druid's Glen resort.

Shortly after the booking was made, a member of staff casually mentioned the unusual transaction to an off-duty garda who was a regular at the hotel's gym. He admitted it was suspicious and agreed to help in whatever way he could. His initial inquiries came up with nothing on either of the names, not even a parking ticket. But when he delved a bit deeper on the garda's Pulse computer system he sent alarm bells ringing across the entire force. The name Kinahan certainly mattered. The wedding of the Dapper Don's son had not been on the police radar and somehow the Kinahan mob had managed to keep a lid on it by using a woman with no links to organised crime to book it. A top-secret emergency meeting was called by the Republic's elite forces and the National Surveillance Unit mounted an operation on the hotel.

Guests dressed to impress on the big day out, sporting their credit cards and mobile phones, felt safe in the knowledge that the wedding had not been picked up by intelligence. On the day, Kinahan Snr looked every inch the Dapper Don when he was pictured as he got out of his chauffeur-driven car, along with the then unknown Jasvinder Singh Kamoo. It was the first sighting of Kinahan in Ireland for years and a big breakthrough in efforts to get a handle on the elusive drug dealer. At the church in Donore Avenue in Dublin, inner-city guests gathered for the most expensive wedding most would ever attend. Following the ceremony, the bride and groom stood on the altar for photographs and posed alongside Kinahan Snr. At the far end of the party stood the Dapper Don's ex-wife, Jean Boylan, along with Marie and George Corish, the parents of the bride, Georgina. In true Godfather style, Kinahan Snr kept his pregnant girlfriend away from the official photographs.

After the formalities the party made their way to the Marriot, where inside guests were dazzled by the ornate candelabra, beautifully set white linen tables, a champagne fountain, silver cutlery and a tiered wedding cake with a cascade of iced roses. During the festivities the Dapper Don kept himself at arm's length from ordinary guests and stayed away from the top table. Unknown to him, specialist equipment including cameras, mobile phone trackers and tech to monitor credit card transactions was being used to build intelligence on the mob. Daniel was photographed alongside Kevin Lynch, an armed robber who had been a close associate of his father for years. Key members of Limerick crime gangs were also snapped along with drug dealers from Northern Ireland and the UK. As the nuptials came to an end the mob packed up and headed back out to Spain, where just one thing stood between them and full control of Puerto Banus – Peter 'Fatso' Mitchell.

Just months after the wedding, Fatso strengthened his position on the Costa when he purchased 'Paparazzi' bar. Its grand opening was attended by the great and the good of the criminal fraternity. The premises, located just a mile outside Puerto Banus beside the Aloha Gardens apartment complex, offered a bar and a restaurant. But it was really a meeting place for drug dealers, including the Kinahans, who met and brokered deals with their customers from all over Europe in the guise of having ordinary business lunches.

They regularly pooled their financial resources and purchased in bulk directly from the producers. Neither Kinahan Snr, nor Cunningham, liked Mitchell so any business done between the two organisations was brokered through Daniel, who was regularly spotted meeting Fatso at the bar. Months after Paparazzi opened for business, surveillance established that Thompson and his cousins Liam and David Byrne were regular visitors along with their father, the ageing fraudster 'Jemmy' Byrne.

In the bar, Fatso was treated like a godfather, having gained the respect that his hard decade in exile on the Costa had earned him. Mitchell had a sense of cunning that came from his impressive longevity in the underworld. He would regularly instruct his hired help in what to say, so his own voice wouldn't be picked up or recorded on the phones. On a typical day Fatso would sit around the bar meeting with a succession of customers with a strict protocol observed. First a drink would be sent to Fatso who would then beckon, or not as the case may be, a would-be customer into his company. With Doyle firmly in Fatso's camp, Thompson and Hutch would regularly go on booze sessions with him, starting their night in the Paparazzi bar. There they would rub shoulders with Russian oligarchs, pick up high-class prostitutes and reminisce on their childhoods in the north inner-city.

Daniel Kinahan wasn't a big drinker and had no interest in partying with Hutch's low-brow pals. He considered himself above most of his underlings and was beginning to see his future at the very top of the drug dealing pile. On February 4th, 2008, Doyle, Hutch and Thompson were sitting in a Jeep at Cancelada, near the Dublin hitman's home. The electricity had suddenly gone off at the property and he had phoned Hutch and told him to collect him, so he could go to the gym while he waited for it to reconnect. They were about to drive away when a BMW pulled up and the passenger started firing shots at Doyle. In an attempt to escape, Hutch slammed his car into a lamppost. Reports from Spain claimed that he and Thompson had to run for their lives, but the gunmen made no attempt to pursue them. Doyle died and Gary Hutch returned home to carry his coffin.

In Spain, investigators blamed the Russian mafia, who they had been told Doyle had fought with during a night out.

Two months later, Fatso Mitchell found himself in a special report across the pages of an Irish newspaper. Furnished with inside information from Spain, photographers had managed to perfectly position themselves in order to snap him meeting with serious players on the drugs scene, including the Byrne brothers and their father James 'Jaws'. The incident was hugely embarrassing for Fatso and lowered him in the eyes of his business partners. Within days of the report, Spanish cops raided his bar and shut it down over 'licensing irregularities'.

A month after the raids the Dapper Don was in Antwerp, Belgium, when cops swooped on him, too, and he found himself at the centre of a major international corruption and money laundering investigation. Kinahan and a Dutch business associate had set up a real estate company in the port city and were planning to convert an old gaming casino into an apartment block. Laws in Belgium meant that Kinahan Snr would be held in custody with no access to bail while the investigation proceeded and he was locked up in the city's main prison on Begijnenstraat.

Belgian cops had been watching Kinahan Snr for some time and had established his connections with some of the most dangerous criminal gangs in Europe, including the Russian mafia and an Israeli drug gang.

The inquiry into Kinahan's money laundering had also established an extraordinary web of corruption involving the organised crime gangs, a local professional soccer club and members of the Belgian police. Following his arrest, local newspapers reported the case as one of the country's worst police corruption scandals ever exposed.

Daniel went to see his father in prison and agreed to take control of business in Spain while his mess was sorted out. As Belgian investigators probed companies as far afield as Pernera in Cyprus, his arrest was conveniently blamed on Fatso and the surveillance on his Paparazzi bar.

In August 2008, three months after Kinahan Snr was nabbed, Fatso was sipping a drink at the El Jaridin Bar, a stone's throw from his own premises, when a hitman in a balaclava ran at him with a gun. Fatso, who despite his nickname was at the peak of his fitness, dived for cover and in the panic the gunman slipped and managed to hit his target just in the shoulder and leg. Two other people sitting nearby were injured.

In hospital, Fatso considered his options. With his bar closed, his home up for sale and his girlfriend terrified, he decided to move to Amsterdam and away from the Costa for good. Very soon another bar replaced Paparazzi as the meeting place for criminals. This time the proprietor was Daniel Kinahan and the bar was called the Auld Dubliner. In control of his father's empire and with his wingman Gary Hutch firmly by his side, the heir to the throne got his first real taste of the power he craved so desperately.

4

Meet the Kinahans

It happened in an instant, just after 4.30am on a Tuesday morning in May 2010, but it had taken two years of intricate planning between crime-fighting forces across the globe.

As dawn broke on the Costa Del Sol, the world awoke to meet the Kinahans. Pictures released later in the day by the Guardia Civil showed heavily-armed police surrounding luxury villas, including one exclusive complex in Estepona where the then 53-year-old Kinahan Snr had been asleep, when the battering rams began to break down his reinforced front door. In the end, the Dapper Don hadn't had time to pull his trousers up and was photographed face first on his bedroom floor in a pair of striped boxer shorts and a T-shirt. It was an image that would be used again and again and one which was a far cry from the suave pictures that existed of Kinahan Snr in tailored linen suits, all primed and ready for the cameras.

The scale of Operation Shovel was a lot to take in, even for those who had followed Kinahan's rise on the Costa. Searches in Spain, the UK and Ireland were conducted simultaneously, and then followed up by raids in Cyprus, Belgium, Dubai and Brazil. Spearheaded by Europol, Operation Shovel had been anchored by the Spanish, due to the mob's presence on the southern coast. In total, almost 750 officers took part in the searches, 31 arrests and follow-up raids.

Kinahan Snr, his sons and Cunningham were all taken into custody along with a string of accountants, solicitors and other associates. Amongst those named amidst the Spanish arrests was the armed robber Kevin Lynch, who had met up with the Dapper Don in prison in Ireland and had moved out to Spain to work as his muscle man. Jasvinder Singh Kamoo, the Indian gentleman who had attended the Irish wedding, was also hauled in along with Denise Kinahan, his sister, and her then partner Gregory Martin. Denise, the youngest of the Kinahan girls, had relocated to the Costa in 2004 after serving on the National Taxi Drivers' Council in Dublin. She had also previously held two joint directorships in Ireland with her nephew, Daniel. The Dapper Don's remaining two sisters had had nothing to do with him for years.

Hardwicke Street mobsters Gary Finnegan and Ross Browning were reeled in too, along with Kinahan associate Anthony Fitzpatrick. Among the premises raided in Spain were the offices of property firm Greenland Securities and the watering hole the Auld Dubliner. In the UK, houses and premises in Slough in Berkshire, Sutton Coldfield in the West Midlands, Westerham in Kent and Oxford, Reading, Canterbury, London and Middlesex were searched. Premises in Tamworth, near Birmingham, where Thomas 'Bomber' Kavanagh's UK operation was based, were also targeted.

In Ireland, the then Garda Commissioner Fachtna Murphy said a clear message had been sent from the operation – that there was no hiding place in the sun. "If people opt to trade drugs and death across borders, police will work together across those borders to address that challenge."

Amongst the treasure trove of information netted during the raids was evidence that €2.5 million had been bet on horse and dog races and football games. The slips for the mainly low odds bets showed that the mob was washing their money in the same way that John Gilligan had previously. Amongst a number of arrests in Ireland was a key Hutch associate and one of the suspects for the spectacular Bank of Ireland robbery just 15 months previously. In Brazil, land at Jacuma was searched and linked to the Greenland offices in Spain. Arrest warrants were issued for Freddie Thompson and Gary Hutch, who were in the Netherlands at the time of the bust.

Spanish police basked in the glory of their coup, declaring they had taken down the Irish mafia and stating that they had recovered more than €500 million in assets. The incredible successes against the Kinahan mob included some jaw-dropping files that suggested they had bought up a corner of Brazil where they were planning to transform 44 hectares into an enormous resort of hundreds of luxury apartments and villas, country clubs, hotels, shops, restaurants and bars.

Two Kinahan-linked companies in Spain and South America were selling the dream. In Spain, Greenland Securities and its director Daniel Kinahan promised a slice of sun-kissed heaven to those who wanted to invest in one of three resorts. The largest, Palma do Mar, had 500 villa plots minutes from a sandy beach and nestled amongst palm trees. An adjacent development called Jardin do Mar had another 100 plots for sale and the third resort, Oasis do Mar, offered 300 completed "luxury villas" at a cost of just under €100,000 each.

The Shovel files named Kamoo as a money launderer for Kinahan and said his firm Negocio Nexo, based in Estepona, traded in commodities as varied as crude oil, cement, fruit, vegetables, olive oil, grain and soya beans. Files handed to a Spanish magistrate also included details of financial interests that Kinahan had in Libya, China, Greece, Panama, several Caribbean Islands, the Cayman Islands, the United States, Switzerland, Liechtenstein and Latvia.

The files listed Michael McAvoy in London as a major business associate of Kinahan. 'Mad' Micky, a notorious UK gangster, was one of the famous Brink's-Mat Robbery gang who stole a record £26 million worth of gold bullion from Heathrow International Trading Estate in 1983. McAvoy stood trial in the Old Bailey and was sentenced to 25 years in prison, but had been released in 2000.

As part of their report to the courts, Spanish police detailed the pyramid-style structure of the Irish mafia and placed Christy Kinahan Snr in pinnacle position. To his right they put Cunningham in charge of trafficking activities and, to his left, Kamoo as his senior money launderer. Directly underneath the trio the report placed the Kinahan boys – Daniel in control of trafficking and 'harsh decisions' while Christopher Jnr managed business and investments for the organisation. The report also highlighted an unidentified female in charge of the business structure in Spain for money laundering and contacts with lawyers and financial institutions – a sort of personal secretary to the Chief Executive. The individual, it stated, collected envelopes of cash for their work at the Auld Dubliner bar.

Under Daniel Kinahan the pyramid continued and Gary Hutch and Freddie Thompson were listed as next in line to the throne. Both were credited with management of drug trafficking, transport and security. Transcripts of phone conversations that had been recorded during the course of the investigation showed that, at one point, the gang discussed purchasing their own container ship to transport drugs into Europe. It seemed the Dapper Don had even suggested that his outfit should buy their own marina in Spain, so they could have a private drug landing port.

Other conversations involved Hutch and Thompson talking about the purchase of weapons, while links were also established between Kinahan and Brian Wright, a cocaine smuggler who had been jailed for 30 years in 2007. Wright had been under investigation in the UK for race fixing by the Jockey Club when a yacht was nabbed as it docked in Cork in southern Ireland.

The boat was packed with 599 kilos of the drug, which at the time, in 1996, was estimated to have a street value of £80 million. Wright was later banned from horse racing premises and people indefinitely, when it was found that he had been involved in widespread corruption of the industry in the 1980s and 1990s. Wright had used betting on racing as a means of money laundering, and a number of jockeys had admitted giving inside information and doping horses at his request. He would then bet £50,000 a time on rigged races and use his winnings to conceal the source of his wealth. Wright, who was nicknamed The Milkman, had been born in Dublin but moved to the UK at the age of 12, growing up in Kilburn.

As praise was heaped on the investigation, Irish gardai remained sceptical for a number of reasons. Firstly, they were very concerned about the amount of officers across different territories who had been briefed about the raids in the days before they happened. Somewhere amidst the hundreds of people who had been fore-warned about the call to arms for the morning of May 26th could have been a paid informant. Kinahan Snr had already bribed cops in Belgium so there was no reason that he wouldn't have others on his books, too.

The length that the investigation had taken had already increased the risk but the mass briefing seemed to be reckless. Such a loose announcement of plans to carry out such a high-level operation would have been unheard of in Ireland or indeed the UK, where officers and specialist units often only found out whose door they were kicking in when they were on the way through them. To add to that problem was the trudging Spanish legal system, which was one of the main reasons that criminals liked to live there so much. In Spain, police hand their investigation files to a magistrate who can take anything from a few days to a few years to go through them. Given the fact that Operation Shovel was two years in the making, it was undoubted that there would be hundreds of thousands of pages of files to get through. And finally, the Kinahans had money. Oodles of it. Their money, Irish cops believed, would buy their freedom as the wheels of justice creaked along.

In the months after the investigation the first indications that the gardai were right, that Kinahan may have been wise to the Spanish police, emerged during an interview with Irish television channel TV3 when a policeman revealed that the mob had put officers under surveillance while they investigated them. Kinahan Snr, the interview revealed, had also had members of his gang trained in military techniques, for confrontations with other gangs and to make sure that they wouldn't break under questioning. The officer who had personally followed Kinahan Snr and members of his gang, including John Cunningham, said Operation Shovel was the biggest investigation his police force had ever been involved in.

"The dismantled organisation represented a very sophisticated group. They used great technological equipment for surveillance and counter-surveillance purposes to detect the presence of the police or the presence of other rival criminal groups that they were up against. They had a very large network of properties which they used to store their illicit products in and to house members of their organisation. The infrastructure used by the dismantled group on the Costa Del Sol was very important, specifically in this jurisdiction. It has not been detected outside the Costa Del Sol," he said.

Kinahan Snr had structured his group exactly like the Italian mafia, the interview revealed. "Taking that word that is recognised internationally as an organised crime gang we could say their infrastructure and activities are very similar to the ones used by the original Italian mafia. So therefore making comparisons between countries instead of the Italian mafia we would call them Irish mafia," the policeman said.

In the interview with journalist Michael Ryan for a documentary called *Ireland's Costa Criminals*, the officer said the investigation was a significant one in Spain against an organised crime outfit. "This would be considered one of the biggest operations that Spanish police have ever been involved in, specifically because of the large number of police involved throughout Europe. So many forces were involved because these individuals moved around Europe a lot. For example, they were in France, Holland and other European countries. The international police cooperation in this operation has been fundamental. The cooperation with the Irish police has been impressive."

A number of things had happened to turn the police attention onto the Kinahans in such a big way. Two years previously, while Kinahan Snr remained in jail in Belgium facing 10 counts of money laundering offences, Europol had finally classified him amongst their most wanted gangsters. Across Europe a number of unsolved gangland murders all seemed to be leading back to the door of the Costa mob and police were increasingly convinced that Paddy Doyle had fallen foul of his own, rather than any Russian mafia.

In Holland, cops were seeing links with the Kinahans and the brutal death of Keith Ennis, whose butchered remains had been discovered stuffed in a suitcase and floating in an Amsterdam canal in February 2009. He was on the run after he had been nabbed with a loaded gun and some Kinahan cocaine. It took Dutch police three weeks to positively identify Ennis' body and they had to post pictures of his decapitated head on their official website as part of their effort to identify him.

Another unsolved case leading back to the Kinahans' door was the disappearance of John 'The Mexican' McKeown, who vanished in 2006 near Torrevieja in Alicante, Spain, shortly after his boss in Ireland, notorious dealer Martin 'Marlo' Hyland, was killed. Hyland was at the top of the gangland ladder in Ireland, having run a huge heroin and cocaine empire for years before he was shot dead as he slept in one of many safehouses he was using. His one-time protégé Eamon 'The Don' Dunne was suspected of ordering the hit to take Hyland out, and the Kinahan mob were suspected of having helped him seize power by removing McKeown as well, to aid the takeover bid.

The disappearance of drug addict Christy Gilroy was also suspicious. It was suspected to have been commissioned by Dunne and handled in Spain by the mob. Dunne had hired Gilroy to carry out a hit, but he'd fled the scene of a murder leaving vital evidence behind, including the weapon, a jacket and a mobile phone. Claiming to have his employee's best interests at heart, Dunne had packaged Gilroy off to Malaga – where he was picked up at Malaga airport by Gary Hutch and brought to a drug treatment clinic in Marbella. Weeks later he was collected from the clinic by another hitman, Eric 'Lucky' Wilson – a gun for hire regularly employed by the mob – and he was never seen again. Wilson was one of the many killers who'd found work within the Kinahan mob when he moved to Spain some years earlier, after a career as an assassin in Ireland. He came from a notorious family of killers back home.

The Wilson brothers Eric, John and Keith were feral and all three had cut their teeth with the drug gang headed by Derek 'Dee Dee' O'Driscoll. While John and Keith were both violent, Eric had been introduced to a major IRA criminal who trained him up at old firing ranges and gave him a trade in killing when he was still in his late teens. At one point during his murderous existence he had compiled a hit list for Thompson, made up of would-be targets from the rival Rattigan gang. On it were the names of Rattigan's sister Sharon, his disabled brother Jason, who has since died, and his then girlfriend Natasha McEnroe.

Suspicions of Kinahan involvement in murders didn't stop at Gilroy's disappearance. When Eamon 'The Don' Dunne was himself murdered, just a month before Operation Shovel, it was clear that he too had fallen foul of the mob. After a honeymoon start to the relationship, things had soured as Dunne's paranoia and trigger-happy tenure threatened to bring heat down on everyone. On the night he was gunned down in the Fassaugh House pub, the chief suspect had just spoken to Daniel Kinahan on the phone.

And it wasn't just murder that was concerning police and had led to the huge operation against the Kinahans. For years, gardai had sought help from their European counterparts to tackle the mob who they *knew* were flooding Ireland and the UK with cocaine, cannabis, heroin and guns, but remained out of their jurisdiction and at arm's length from the law. Despite these constant requests for help with their inquiries, the Irish had remained at the back of the queue in Spain, as the threats from other mafia were deemed greater. But by 2008, the unchallenged Kinahan Snr and his crew had become so powerful that the scale of their operation was causing shockwaves.

In February of that year, just months after the ill-planned wedding in Ireland, a bogus pasta-importing firm was busted in Kildare in the Irish midlands and former Leeds footballer Eddie Van Boxtel had gone on the run while on bail after being nabbed with drugs. Follow-up searches had led officers to a warehouse where it was discovered that up to 20 pasta shipments had gone through the premises in the 12 months before the raid. That gave the 'pasta' smuggling ring a potential street value of more than €100 million in just one year. Gardai again went to their European counterparts – and this time the Kinahans had become big enough to matter. The Spanish, Dutch and British police finally got on board.

Kinahan Snr had become paranoid after the gardai discovered his second major route and barked orders at his crew to change their movements and be careful they weren't being watched. Despite his orders, most of the pumped-up enforcers and associates continued to do the same thing every day. In a scene played out with the regularity of clockwork, they showed up at the Centro Plaza to start their day in the Plaza gym below. Then it was on to an upstairs café for lunch, before meeting up later in the pubs and bars of the bustling town for nights of drinking and cocaine.

While he had always been concerned about his security, just as Operation Shovel was launched Kinahan Snr set about making sure that no cracks had developed in his system. The gang increased the amount of vehicles they used to move around in and largely leased high-powered cars, using them for often just one day in order to avoid detection. Key players were ordered to move around more and only use specially-adapted encrypted mobile phones for any business calls they had to make or take. Those phones were regularly destroyed after use despite costing €2,000 a piece.

In the days after Shovel, the Kinahans, Cunningham and their associates were brought one by one before the Spanish courts. Each was questioned individually by Judge Maria Carmen Gutierrez Hanares, who released most on bail but committed the top men to prison to await trial.

Following his arrest in Spain, Sally Anne Kinahan, the then Assistant General Secretary of the ICTU, made her one and only statement about her brother, in which she revealed that she hadn't spoken to him in 30 years: "I am deeply shocked and distressed at the revelations of recent days and it is something that I am now trying to come to terms with. I have had no relationship with this person for almost 30 years. While it is necessary to let the legal process run its course without prejudice, it goes without saying that I am extremely conscious of the impact that such activity has on the most vulnerable in society and it is something which I condemn unreservedly. That is all I have to say on the matter and I will be making no further comment."

The statement, while brief, was an interesting insight into how the collateral damage of the Dapper Don's career choice had divided even his own family. Behind bars at Alhaurin de la Torre Prison near Malaga, Kinahan Snr met with his lawyers and six months after their arrest John Cunningham, Christopher and Daniel Kinahan were released on strict bail conditions. They had to sign on to an Estepona court once a week and surrender their passports. For the Dapper Don, it wasn't so simple. He was initially released and then re-arrested, as he was still facing his money laundering conviction in Belgium. But while his father manoeuvred his way through his difficult legal position, Daniel took charge of the mob's repositioning in Europe and the all-important image that it was 'business as usual'. Despite the huge damage that had been done to the Irish mafia, they were intent on putting a positive spin on the arrests in order to placate customers, so they wouldn't be tempted to switch allegiances.

While Daniel organised a big knees-up in the Auld Dubliner, his father ordered his henchmen to leak stories that he was confident he would beat all the charges and that he would be back up and running in no time. Financially they had to recoup their losses. Like any corporate entity facing financial collapse, they would have to make cuts and hard decisions. In the Netherlands, Hutch worked flat out to keep the show on the road as things began to settle down. A year after the arrests, the Dapper Don was flown out of Madrid in handcuffs after he agreed to be extradited. One month later, Thompson was arrested in Dublin and brought before the courts because of the Spanish extradition warrant, which stated that he was wanted as a member of a criminal gang involved in drugs and arms trafficking.

Thompson had the audacity to seek free legal aid, but the State lawyers objected on the grounds that he freely travelled to and from the jurisdiction, was not registered for tax and was not in receipt of social welfare. Thompson's counsel John Berry argued to no avail that his client has been supported by his mother, street trader Christina, and that the €20,000 compensation he had received in road accident claims had been spent. During the case the High Court heard that during a two-year period when he had been under surveillance he had been to Morocco and Amsterdam on numerous occasions. Eventually losing his battle, Thompson enjoyed a free flight to Malaga, where he was quickly bailed and joined his pals in Puerto Banus. With the lads from Dublin together again on the Costa, it seemed it was party time again.

5

Love Hate

All of a sudden the penny seemed to drop with estate agent 'Sondra'. "Harry Redknapp is selling his penthouse property. Maybe you would like to zee zat?" she whispered to me, her left eyebrow raised with cheeky abandon.

"Ooooh, Nigel," I squealed. "Isn't he married to the model? Louise?"

Journalist Mick McCaffrey raised his head from the mobile phone he was talking into and looked at me, bored. "No that's his son ye fuckin eejit but I'd be interested in tha'. How much is Redknapp lookin' for?"

At €970,000, having dropped the price from €1.2 million, we were assured that Redknapp was practically giving it away. It was the summer of 2013 and we were at Torre Bermaja on Estepona's so-called Golden Mile, fresh off the plane from Ireland posing as 'Nidge and Trish', two characters in a gritty crime drama called Love Hate that had become hugely popular on Irish television. In the show Nidge, a psychotic drug boss, rules his turf with violence while indulging in prostitutes and copious amounts of cocaine. He loves to flash his cash while Trish, his gangster's moll, is happy to turn a blind eye to his sins for the sake of a pair of Louboutin heels.

There is no doubt but Torre Bermeja is exclusive in the extreme. The terracotta residences of rich Russians, Americans and Europeans stand almost Disney-like in manicured gardens. There are a few for weekly holiday rental – if you have a spare €5,000 in your back pocket. Sitting on a private beachfront, each has their own terraces facing every way the sun shines, complete with hot tubs overlooking the sparkling Mediterranean. There are two large outdoor pools serviced all day by waiting staff, and a huge indoor pool with sparkly lights and a gym.

While Torre Bermaja has been home to perfectly innocent residents from all over the world, it was also at this complex where Spanish police bypassed the strict security and bulldozed their way through the bulletproof door of penthouse 1501 to arrest Christy Kinahan Snr in May 2010. It was here where he was filmed face down on the floor of his bedroom in a pair of underpants and a T-shirt.

It was to this exclusive complex where he returned after he'd finally got bail and it was here, on a melting hot day, that a couple had watched him playing with his young children in the communal swimming pool. In a temper after taking a mobile phone call, they would later tell us, he ducked them under the water, holding them for those few seconds too long until on-lookers began to shift uncomfortably in their sun chairs. Later, after his extradition to Belgium and a short sentence for money laundering, he returned to Torre Bermeja and was often spotted strolling through the well-tended gardens with his young wife and family.

Pulling up at the complex, I had only just stepped out of the air-conditioned car when I could feel the make-up I had applied in an effort to glam up start to slide around on my face. Red faced or not, we were a classic gangland couple. McCaffrey in a designer baseball cap had four mobile phones on the go from the minute we stepped out of our high-spec rental, remaining distracted and uninterested at all times. I towered and sweated in silver wedge sandals and clothes more fitting for a nightclub. 'Trashy' Trishy with Nidge's drug money burning a hole in her pocket and two layers of fake eyelashes. It was a bit of black humour on our part, but amazingly we pulled it off and the fact that we didn't give a second name or email address and were accompanied by a bizarre Spanish man with a camera around his neck seemed to bypass both the estate agent and the highly-trained security guards. It seemed to me that when it came to Costa real estate, money talks.

It would be hard for an ordinary tourist to understand the influence the Kinahan mob held on the Costa by 2013 – three years after Operation Shovel had vowed that the Irish mafia had been dismantled.

Far from being shut down, they had grown like never before and in the huge gated villas, in the bustling restaurants and in pubs, clubs and businesses they had spread their tentacles and influence to such an extent that the Costa and the area around Puerto Banus had become their absolute seat of power. Operation Shovel had not closed them down, it had empowered them.

Acting on inside information, we were in Spain to try to

get up close and personal with the mob in whatever way we could and to do so we had entered the belly of the beast in order to understand just how far Kinahan, his sons and their army of friends from Oliver Bond, Hardwicke Street and the north inner-city had come. Luckily, there were a number of properties on view at Torre Bermeja described in the brochures as a 'breathtakingly luxurious complex'.

"This is the most secure and exclusive complex on the Costa," the estate agent assured us as she walked us through the gated entrance and in to see the €1.4 million penthouse apartment up for sale.

"There are four security guards monitoring each complex 24/7."

The penthouse, located in a block beside Kinahan Snr's bolt hole, was a carbon copy of his pad. I had never seen anything quite like it. A huge entrance hall led into a vast living area complete with a dining table to sit 15 and two huge terraces kitted out with full outdoor kitchens. Up a grand staircase a massive double room opened out from the hall, while a master bedroom complete with a bath that looked more like a swimming pool, set beneath a plasma screen television, overlooked another terrace.

Trish was impressed, but it just wasn't 'pink' enough. While Nidge didn't like the furnishings. As we took in the views our photographer friend broke free and made his way towards the Dapper Don's property, where he settled down into a bush outside. We later spotted a plume of smoke rising from said bush but seemed to be only ones that noticed.

In the second penthouse the third bedroom had been transformed into an office, which definitely didn't do it for us.

Drug dealers do not need offices unless they are for laundering money, but of course we didn't say that quite so bluntly.

Outside we wandered through the tropical gardens, constantly monitored by CCTV. The rich residents ambled by; nannies wheeled babies in prams and Lamborghinis, Bentleys and Mercedes drove in and out of underground car parks. Each property was fitted with a high-spec alarm system and each room had its own panic button, we were told. Services on hand 24 hours a day included the security guards who patrolled the premises and logged everyone coming and going. It struck me as ironic to think that the Dapper Don had once convinced a judge that he was a struggling heroin addict, securing for himself a free education that had formed part of this twisted rags-to-riches story.

Torre Bermeja reminded me of the Brazilian development that Kinahan Snr was planning to build on the north-east coastline of South America, where we had sent a local reporter to have a look. Operation Shovel billed it as a €200-500 million development, but instead we had found a barren wasteland where not a sod of earth had been turned. The brochures had sold it as a slice of sun-kissed heaven, a luxury villa complex with restaurants and swimming pools on a gentle hill with views down to the perfect sandy beaches of the South Atlantic. Instead it was a debris-strewn patch – with for-sale signs slapping in the breeze. Initially set to be completed in 2010, the Brazilian dream appeared to be all but over.

"It is dead in the water," a local estate agent had told our man. "There was some initial excavation done years ago, but after that there was nothing. The fact that another development directly in front of it opened in 2012 was just the final nail in the coffin. There is a concrete wall now where the view would have been."

Where the development was to be, our reporter had found signs from no less than three different estate agents adorning windswept palm trees. One read: "Land financing. Sign for just R$3,000" – implying that parcels of land were being sold for a down payment of less than €1,000. Apart from that, the only signs of work were found in a small corner that had been excavated and there was an unpaved, unevenly curbed, dirt track. Debris, rocks and rubbish were strewn everywhere. Elsewhere in the town, located in the state of Paraiba in Brazil's historically poor north-east region, there was little to suggest development, just unpaved roads, ramshackle houses, horses and carts. I wondered how many investors had been stung by the promise of quick money.

I snapped back to reality and to the face of Sondra, who anxiously led us ever onwards through the complex. It was like being on an episode of 'A Place In The Sun' and the hope etched on Sondra's innocent face was making me feel really guilty. On reflection I decided that it was our non-commital, clear disappointment with the previous properties that had secured us the invite to see Harry Redknapp's place which was furnished, Sondra told us, in Fendi from top to bottom. I lifted a vase and peaked underneath to find the price tag still attached – €730.

"For a vase, Nigel. Can ya believe it?" I said in my best Dublin accent beaming at my discovery.

"We'll think about it – if he throws in the 'Fendeee', maybe," said McCaffrey.

I stuck my head into one of the very expensive kitchen

cupboards, so as not to be seen laughing. We eventually left, having had our fun. We were on the Costa for much more serious things and we needed to stay focused and alert.

We travelled next to Benahavis to see the luxury villa where Christopher Jnr had been living with Georgina Corish, who he had married at the Marriot Hotel. We'd seen the pictures, the family snaps of the Corish family, beaming with happiness high in the hills of San Pedro de Alcantara overlooking the Spanish coast. In the photograph's sisters Georgina, Layla, Stephanie and Rachel were all done up to party in their designer dresses, high heels and with sun-kissed tans, hair extensions, manicures and facials. Parents Marie Corish, a factory worker, and unemployed Georgie stood proudly beside their brood. They'd come a long way from working-class Rialto in Dublin, I thought.

In one picture it was Rachel's 30th birthday and the family were joined by some of their oldest friends from Dublin. Those who couldn't afford to make the trip had been brought out free of charge. Despite my staunch stance against drug money and all that goes with it, I couldn't help but see the hardship on their faces and understand why such a trip was too hard to resist. There was the sun, the expensive hotel and the lure of that escape of feeling rich, just for a little while.

In the pictures, thousands of euros worth of champagne lay open and discarded, fine wines were left half drunk and cocktails in every colour lined the tables. Georgina beamed for the cameras with more than one reason to celebrate. Surrounded by her family and friends, the former council worker had just given birth to her second child and to please her father-in-law, she had named the baby 'Sonny' after Vito

Corleone's eldest in the fictional masterpiece The Godfather. A small gesture perhaps but it was all thanks to the Dapper Don and his international drugs, money laundering and weapons operation, that the glitz and glam of the celebrations were possible.

Outside the gates and out of view of the security cameras it looked like there was plenty of space in the gated villa for a growing family. A massive outdoor swimming pool enjoyed the beautiful views of the coast below and the house was clearly fitted with the best fixtures and fittings that money could buy. Georgina, and by association her sisters, had reached the hallowed grounds of the Kinahan inner circle – they were family. Other pictures we unearthed during our investigation showed them whiling away their days on Puerto Banus' private beaches, where they could sip champagne without a care in the world, party at the plush Ocean Club and pose beside the yacht they often chartered so that they could sunbathe at sea like top celebrities.

The Corish family weren't the only ones to be lured by the wealth that the Kinahans had to offer. Days later, nearer the coast, our surveillance team spotted Kinahan's ex Jean Boylan, who a contact told us had relocated along with her partner Harry Mallon to Spain. Sinead, a half sister to the Kinahan boys and her partner Stephen Johnson, had moved out, too.

Our investigations took us on to Vista Golf, the home of retired bankers, property developers and other successful professionals, where Gary Hutch and Daniel Kinahan had been regularly spotted and where a number of Kinahan safe houses were identified by Operation Shovel. Onwards to La Alzambra Hill Club, home to other mob members, and then to meet with another contact who showed us just how carefree those who'd been arrested during the crackdown had become.

Denise Kinahan, he said, had become a celebrated Marbella socialite and a key guest at all the extended mob events. Known as the life and soul of the parties, she was so far removed from her respectable sisters back home that it was hard to fathom they had all been reared together, under the same roof. Her brother, the Dapper Don, was far less sociable and was rarely seen with the underlings from his gang. In fact he remained an aloof figure who spoke to few and only went out to eat in some of Marbella's most expensive restaurants. In a tiny café we were given pictures of Denise dancing on a table at a pal's wedding and quaffing champagne. Far from lying low, we find, most of the mob and their wags are regulars at the Ocean Club, posh La Sala restaurant, Tibu nightclub, Linekers and the Portside bar in Puerto Banus.

Outside the town in what looked like an underground car park was the new gym, where we were told the mob now liked to gather. We made our way to have a look and saw a big MGM sign outside, along with the name of the boxer Matthew Macklin above the door. Our enquiries told us that nobody would be seen at the Plaza gym anymore and, with the Auld Dubliner closed down, a little pub above the gym, Slainte Bar, had become the popular after-session hangout.

We set up our cameras and waited and watched. As we trawled through what we could find online we discovered that when Macklin opened the doors of the facility in 2012 it was with great pomp and ceremony – he even hired bikini clad models for the occasion. The European champion, known as the 'Tipperary Tornado', even made the society pages on the Costa Del Sol for his non-profit making venture, set up to help fund a local charity for children with special needs and which vowed to open its facilities to impoverished youths.

Macklin had never made any secret of his friendship with Daniel Kinahan, who'd travelled the world with him for years and was a regular in his dressing room pre-fight. Macklin had been introduced to Kinahan back in Dublin through a mutual acquaintance called Joey 'The Lips' O'Brien, an amateur boxer who had been a teenage street dealer for Freddie Thompson. O'Brien had met Macklin at a boxing tournament and the pair had hit it off becoming close pals. At one point O'Brien had moved to Birmingham along with his pal James Quinn and enjoyed legendary nights out with Macklin and boxer Ricky Hatton. Kinahan was immediately impressed with Macklin when they first met and was bowled over by his celebrity. O'Brien, too, had remained friends with the boxer until his luck took a turn for the worst and he wound up at the centre of the gangland murder of drug dealer John 'Champagne' Carroll, who was shot dead while socialising in Grumpy Jack's Pub in Dublin in 2009. O'Brien ended up on the witness protection programme after agreeing to give evidence against those involved in the assassination and had gone to ground ever since. But Macklin and Kinahan's relationship had blossomed and the pair had become firm friends.

Macklin's brother, Seamus, was always by his side and knocked around with lots of the young Dubliners on the fringes of the organisation. Even the Dapper Don was a fan and had cheered him on at numerous fights. Back when criminal Eamon Dunne was causing mayhem in the underworld in Dublin with his trigger-happy assassins, Kinahan Snr had attempted to call a ceasefire and organised a summit for criminals, purchasing 50 ringside seats for the Macklin fight at the National Stadium in Dublin. When he couldn't go he'd sent Daniel along to host the no-expense-spared night attended by major gangland figures including Thompson, Dunne and Brian O'Reilly. But there was something more than just a friendship when it came to the gym and in the run-up to the opening we could see that it was Daniel Kinahan who had been dealing with the builders on a twitter site, @djk256, which we believed belonged to him.

It seemed extraordinary that Matthew Macklin would go into business with Kinahan while Operation Shovel and the drugs and weapons charges were still looming, but the facts were there and nobody seemed to be hiding 'Danny's' involvement with the place.

On MGM's Facebook site it was clear the gym was also being used by enforcers and key lieutenants of Kinahan's mob. We trawled through the postings and saw Gary Finnegan and Kevin Lynch working out. We knew Finnegan from old as he was Daniel's very own guard dog who patrolled his turf in Dublin and travelled back and forth to Spain at his master's bidding. The pair had been friends for years and we'd been told before that Finnegan, who'd been arrested but never charged with the Dunne shooting, was unwaveringly loyal to Daniel and had introduced his cousin, Barry Finnegan, and his pal, Ross Browning, into the fold.

On the Facebook page we spotted a photograph of Christopher Jnr's sick child, Georgia, hanging above the reception at the newly opened gym and we watched footage of a recent event with Daniel himself taking to the ring. Macklin seemed oblivious to the serious reputations of those around him and had posed for pictures with Dean Howe and Liam Brannigan, key players in the Crumlin Drimnagh feud and cousins of Thompson and the Byrnes, who played a major role in the distribution network of drugs into Dublin. The gym appeared to be courting celebrity as well as gangsters. Pictures showed the Olympic star Katie Taylor with her father and then trainer Pete, who had visited it and sparred in the top-of-the-range rings. Frank Bruno, too, had paid a visit.

We'd become increasingly paranoid working on the Costa, and particularly as the mob had re-emerged from the ashes of Shovel. I'd been out to the south coast of Spain a number of times since the arrests, but things had seemed to get darker each time. On the first occasion I had travelled over to try to talk to the Kinahans, after they had finally secured bail following months in prison. As part of the conditions they had to sign on at court number three in Estepona every Monday morning, so it was the perfect opportunity to try to get an interview if they were interested in talking.

The court was on a narrow enough street that didn't seem to see much action. I had arrived early and tucked myself into a doorway, hoping they would go in and sign their bail bond and that I could approach them when they came out. I saw the judge arriving, a young female magistrate who parked her own car and walked up the street by herself. It seemed odd to me that a judge on such a high-profile, organised crime case was so open at the courtroom. In Ireland, our Special Criminal Court judges who are charged with hearing cases about subversive and organised crime are given police escorts to and from the building when they are sitting. They are driven right into the court buildings and are only seen by the public when they appear in the body of the courtroom. But I supposed in Spain things were done differently and magistrates can often be years examining police files before a trial even begins.

Christopher Jnr had arrived first wearing a hat and in no mood to talk. He sped past me and up the street to a waiting car. Daniel came next in his signature designer baseball cap. He signed in but raced out the door and away from me to the top of the road. I waited for the Dapper Don but he didn't come. I waited and waited and at one point I saw a vintage gold-coloured Jaguar circle the roundabout at the top of the road and I just about made out someone who looked a bit like him. But the car never stopped and then the judge came out, walked back to her car and drove off and the security guard locked up the courtroom and went for his siesta.

During a phone call later I was assured that Kinahan Snr had signed on, but I hadn't seen him and I wondered had he forged some sweetheart deal with the court. On that occasion I'd had some time to spare before my flight home so I headed out to Daniel's home, a terracotta villa in an exclusive neighbourhood somewhere off the motorway near Estepona. It was walled and surrounded by security cameras but I knocked none the less and was surprised when a Spanish woman pulled open the gate. "Sir Daniel, not here," she said. "Later, later." Sir Daniel? Surely that was the language barrier and not how he chose to be referred to by his staff. Within minutes I could see we were being tailed by two young guys in a Volkswagen Golf. We drove around the residential streets and eventually out onto the motorways and lost them. I made my way to the Auld Dubliner, located in one of those shopping centre complexes off the main road. I just wanted to have a look. It was very ordinary and some tourists sat outside, so I took a seat and ordered a glass of beer. Inside, three burly bare-chested men stood at the bar. They looked like boxers. And seconds later, the same Volkswagen Golf started to circle and I just got the sense that anything could happen and that being a journalist certainly did not guarantee my safety.

When we were planning for the job in 2013 we suspected the Kinahans had invested heavily in all sorts of enterprises around southern Spain, so we booked nothing for ourselves through the newspaper company. Instead of rooms in a hotel, we had booked a private rental from a trusted source, so our location would remain secret should anything occur while we were there. Cars would be swapped every day and everyone wore an alarm and worked in pairs. We were still close enough to Puerto Banus to stroll down to the port and try to mingle with the other tourists and that's what we did, to get some cover while we watched and waited.

Puerto Banus is the playground of hedonism, where the mega rich party and others sell their souls to join in. A heady mix of money, cocaine and sex swirl around in a melting pot of drug dealers, oligarchs and rich entrepreneurs who preen themselves in designer clothes. Located about 10 kilometres from Marbella, 'Banus' is known as the St Tropez of Andalucia. Super yachts moor up in its marina, overlooked by a strip of bars, restaurants and designer boutiques. Beach clubs famous for their champagne spray parties flank the port, while 45 minutes away sits the rock of Gibraltar, famed for its macaque monkeys and its reputation as a money laundering mecca.

Plenty of regular tourists visit Puerto Banus. They wander

around, white legged, holding children's hands and gaze at the yachts and the super cars like Ferraris, Lamborghinis and Bentleys that cruise along the port. Women who look like supermodels in high heels teeter along, too, beside pumped-up men, tattooed and muscular. By day, paella and seafood is served to diners who vie for tables with a view. At night, the families go home and the port comes alive as international DJs appear at the super clubs and music blares from the hip rooftop bars which open from dusk to dawn. Cocktails and champagne flow and the drug dealers who flood Europe with mountains of cocaine whisper in the shadows.

Finally, our team spotted the Dapper Don and, despite all his money, counter surveillance training and round-the-clock security, he didn't even know that we'd nabbed him on his own turf.

The image of Kinahan Snr relaxed and tanned, tossing raw fish into his mouth at a portside Sushi bar would be a rare glimpse of the head of the Irish mafia where he felt most comfortable, and it would be an image that would become iconic for so many reasons.

Our investigations had been fruitful, not least realising the significance of MGM and its links to the Kinahan mob, but reeling in the big fish was the cherry on top. Up until that evening, in Puerto Banus, Kinahan had only ever been photographed going in or out of a courtroom – apart from one dog-eared old mugshot which had found its way out of the garda files in the days before an inquiry would be launched about it. The result was that Kinahan had been the master of his own image, and expecting to be photographed at courtrooms he had always dressed in suits, surrounded himself

CLASH OF THE CLANS

with teams of lawyers and looked for all the world like the businessman he liked to portray himself as.

For days we had baked under the Spanish sun hoping our contacts would come good and finally they had – Christy had come out to play in the exact spot we had been told he would. It was an exhilarating evening in the world of the lowly crime journalist, and myself and McCaffrey were thrilled. We had watched as he pulled into the port driving a large black Mercedes, one of the countless cars he changed every few days to avoid surveillance from the police. We saw him as he took out his port card, an entry ticket costing €3,000 a season that allows the elite few to cruise the strip in their flash cars and park up beside the million-euro yachts that dock on the marina. He looked good. Fit, tanned and wearing designer casuals. Inside the Sushi bar we watched as he was greeted like a celebrity and settled in to sit with an associate while watching the leggy beauties of Puerto Banus go by.

For an instant an altercation nearby grabbed his attention, when members of the Guardia Civil intervened in a dispute. Our powerful camera lenses captured something – a look which Kinahan gave the uniformed officers, a look of pure hatred.

We watched as he drank only water with his meal and then went into a neighbouring bar, where he again was greeted in a manner befitting the Godfather he had become. Punters stood to attention, extending their hands and offering him their seats and while he was friendly, he was not in the mood to settle down. We had been warned about Kinahan's spotters and noticed one watching just outside the restaurant where he dined. We watched him watching everyone that walked up and down near his master, noting every car, every face that came within a hair's breath of the Dapper Don. It was late when he left the port, driving the Mercedes himself and taking off at breakneck speed out into the labyrinth of motorway that lies just outside.

We should have known to leave after him, happy with our lot, but we'd got what we came for and surely we deserved a celebratory drink. We reasoned there was no harm in having the one. At the Portside Bar we joined our team and sat discreetly in a corner, where we could keep an eye on the goings on. Amidst the hundreds of revellers that were out on the Costa we reckoned we looked like any other group of tourists enjoying a heady night of summer. There were Irish and Brits everywhere, girls dressed to the nines with unnaturally long lashes – and dealers, too, trailing the bars with man-bags of ecstasy and cocaine.

In an instant, one of our team noticed a guy watching me and followed him to the bathroom where he heard him on the phone.

"Nicola Tallant and the *Sunday World* are here. Get down here now," he overheard him say.

We needed to move.

"Separate, go now."

We left in different directions and the next few minutes are like the scene from a movie, but it's real and there is danger.

Our own watchers followed us discreetly as we made our way through the laneways and cobbled alleys of Puerto Banus, doubling back a few times and turning at the last minute as we arrived at the entrance to the port. Our surveillance team watched the spotters as they followed us, all the while on their mobile phones arranging for back-up. At the entrance, we managed to lose them and disappear into the crowds, travelling separately back to our accommodation. I arrived first.

"Where the fuck is McCaffrey?" I asked, just as a taxi pulled up and he bounded out.

"How did that happen?" He was stunned, too. "They were behind me, shouting at me. I just kept going. Saw this taxi at the gates and just jumped in. Poor fucker didn't know what was going on. I gave him a tip. Who was that young lad in the Portside?"

The photographers took off their body cameras and started to upload the images they'd captured. I poured us all a drink and we got to work identifying who they were and risk-assessing the situation that we had just found ourselves in. We quickly confirmed our suspicions and we were not being paranoid. The men who had followed us were right at the heart of the Kinahan empire, chief associates of Daniel Kinahan and pumped-up enforcers who were at his bidding. We were right about one thing – when Kinahan Snr is around, his inner circle were never far behind.

"Right, Tallant, you're blown. It's the sunbeds for you from here on in," the lads decided.

That was fair enough and I wasn't going to argue, the fact that they had recognised me had almost compromised the whole job and put all our lives in danger. Days later, McCaffrey was spotted again, and it was an even closer shave. This time Kinahan's heavies had back-up and the only card in his hand was alert and calm movement through the crowds and to safety. The thugs shouted after him: "We'll kill you, you dirty *Sunday World* scum."

As we neared the end of our surveillance work, I went to the port during the day. We'd got what we came for so there was no problem if I was seen and I just wanted to do a few quick pieces to camera for a video we were making before we left. As we filmed, I noticed a guy standing behind the cameraman clearly making a call on a mobile phone. Something about him made me nervous, so we moved and set up elsewhere. "Just a few more minutes and I will get it right," I assured my colleagues as I screwed up the lines again and again.

With that came the man again, but this time I knew him as the bloke we'd photographed with the Dapper Don eating Sushi some nights previous. We had no idea who he was, but he looked Moroccan. He strolled past me and averted his eyes as he reached for his mobile phone in his hand. He tried to look casual but there was nothing random about what he was doing.

I watched him watching me and realised it was time to go.

6

Boxing Clever

The tweet was simple and accompanied with a picture of a guy in boxing gloves and covered in sweat. '@marvinherbert2 looking happy this morning whilst training,' it read. The date was July 31st, 2013.

I'd become accustomed to throwing an eye over the activities at the MGM boxing club since our investigation into the Irish mafia in Spain had led us to the facility outside Puerto Banus. I suppose you could call it creeping, but many an interesting character had shown up, none more so than Marvin Herbert. I just knew the name was familiar from the moment I saw it on the twitter account of Ian Dixon, a cousin of Daniel Kinahan who was fighting under the MGM black and gold and training intermittently in Puerto Banus. I punched it into Google and within seconds a series of headlines gave me a glimpse at the history of a career criminal.

Herbert had been a heavy for hire and a feared enforcer, first in the UK and later on the Costa, where he had run into all sorts of trouble. He had first been called a 'premier league' criminal by a judge, when he was jailed for being part of a 'Yardie hit-squad' in the early 2000s. On his release he had moved to Spain, where he had set up some sort of business offering 'security' for bars around Puerto Banus. On a street outside a coffee shop in 2009 he'd had an altercation and been shot a number of times in broad daylight. By all accounts it was a miracle he had survived, but he had lost an eye and spent months in hospital recovering. Since then, he'd been referred to in gangland circles as 'one eyed Marv', but instead of going to ground after his brush with death he had gone back to a life of crime and was arrested in 2011 in Spain over an attack on a man who had suffered a broken leg.

What was of even more interest was that he had also been linked to the Dale Cregan case and was wanted by UK police.

Cregan was notorious in the UK where he had just started a life sentence without parole. He had pleaded guilty the previous February to the murder of two female police officers, Nicola Hughes and Fiona Bone, who had gone to investigate a 999 call about a burglary. The call was later found to have been made by Cregan, who had led them into a trap. At the time he was on bail for the murder of Mark Short and his father David and cops suspected that Herbert and others had helped him lay low. Clearly, Herbert had no problem sparring at Macklin's gym despite the fact that he had been linked to the Cregan case, but weeks after he'd posed for the tweeted photograph he was arrested at the gym and found himself before a Spanish judge fighting extradition back to the UK.

MGM politely ignored the goings on and continued to host boxing celebrities at every available opportunity, posting videos and photographs of their coaches, including the dangerous heavy Lynch, Christy Snr's jailhouse pal, enforcer and trainer of young children in the skills of boxing. Despite the criminal calibre of many of those involved, the gym appeared to be going from strength to strength in its first year or so of business.

One of the events I stumbled upon while trawling through the MGM social media pages was a charity bash which had taken place in Spain. It was a 'white collar' boxing night, during which Daniel and his brother Christopher Jnr had taken to the ring themselves at the H2O hotel. Daniel had won on points and was cheered rather loudly. Amongst those in attendance were ex-footballer Graeme Souness and former world boxing champion Frank Bruno.

I noticed the date of the event, which told another story. That Daniel had fought it out despite news that one of his best friends and associates, Jason Carroll, had just been gunned down in Dublin the night before. Carroll, a drug dealer, was under investigation by the Criminal Assets Bureau at the time despite trying to hide his criminal activities through his work as a bread delivery man. It had evidently been a big night and clearly Daniel was the star of the show. His reputation and popularity in the criminal underworld seemed to be growing all the time so I decided to see who had taken the trip to Spain to see him perform in the ring and found out that a host of top-ranking criminals from Dublin had travelled, including Martin 'the Viper' Foley, and Michael Cunningham, the brother of Kinahan's right hand man John, who had met them at Malaga airport. The Byrne brothers and their father, Jaws, had also made the trip along with their associates from the UK.

Trawling through social media tags for the gym, I then

discovered that MGM had come in for some attention from the boxer Jamie Kavanagh, who publicly thanked them for sponsoring his fight in the US. Amongst those tagged for praise in Kavanagh's tweet was the handle @djk256, the same Twitter site we had worked out belonged to Daniel Kinahan. While Kavanagh had become a pretty famous boxer and was tipped for great success, he was also the son of Gerard 'Hatchet' Kavanagh, Bomber's cousin and business partner, who was by then a long-term resident of Benalmadena, located 50 kilometres down the coast from Marbella.

Jamie, a lightweight boxer, had turned professional in 2009, when he moved to Los Angeles and started training under the legendary Freddie Roach. The youngster had enjoyed an impressive career under Roach, but had moved to the Joel Diaz camp. Frank Bruno had tagged MGM, too, when he'd sparred at the gym along with the former boxer turned match presenter 'Big' Joe Egan. Egan was liked throughout the boxing world and was firm friends with The Monk. Others had no connections whatsoever to Ireland and just appeared to show up to have a look around the gym if they were visiting the Costa.

Clearly there were clever marketeers working for the premises who drew in celebrity visitors in their droves. Evander Holyfield was photographed with Dixon in the ring while he was visiting Puerto Banus with a charity run by Canadian philanthropist Yank Barry. British professional boxer Tommy Coyle tweeted after a short break to Spain: "Carlsberg don't do gyms but if they did…" The real star of the show was the face of MGM.

Macklin, who was training hard under the tutelage of his coach, Jamie Moore, had moved out to Spain from Salford as his old pal made a last-ditch bid at fame. Under Moore he was getting ready for a fight in Atlantic City. Fans of the boxer were hoping that he would show America he could still go for a world title when he took on Willie Nelson. Macklin was on the back foot after a defeat in the ring, but clearly hadn't given up his dream, and with the fight due to be screened live on HBO it was a huge deal to him. A win on primetime TV would surely put him back on the map. Sky Sports Boxing travelled to Spain to interview him and Moore at the MGM premises, showcasing the new facility at the same time.

Back in Ireland, crime writers wrote how Christy Kinahan Snr's Irish mafia was weighing in behind their favourite boxer as he planned to fly Stateside, while boxing correspondents concentrated on the upcoming fight. "Mob out in force to support Macklin," ran headlines in the news pages, while "Macklin's US dream," was the more toned-down story for sport, where analysis of the fight made no reference to organised crime. It was strange to say the least, and it seemed to me that any other sport would be horrified by such blatant links with organised crime, but nobody in the boxing world seemed to bat an eyelid. Even the boxing journalists seemed to be trained to ignore the elephant in the room.

I wasn't naïve, the links between boxing and organised crime had been well and truly documented. For anyone who had any doubts about the mob's influence on the sport, there was Sammy 'The Bull' Gravano's testimony at the Dirksen Senate Office Building on Constitution Avenue in Washington DC in 1993. There, he had told the hearing how the Gambino family had been involved in boxing throughout the 1960s, and how he had regularly attended fights with mob boss John Gotti.

The one-time underboss turned State witness told the gathered US senators that he had got to know a heavyweight named Renaldo Snipes, who he had hoped to set up in a fight with the undefeated WBO champion Francesco Damiani. In the hearing, Gravano claimed that Damiani was 'with' an organised crime family in Italy, and that they had come to New York to discuss the possibility of a fight with Snipes. "One of the things I did was try to reach out and set up a meeting with a guy who was in charge of boxing for Donald Trump. I met with him in Atlantic City and he said a fight between the two would sell. It would be even bigger if Snipes had a higher ranking with one of boxing's sanctioning bodies," he said.

Gravano went on to describe how he met with a named referee in Las Vegas, who said he could get Snipes up the ranking for a cut-price fee of $5,000 as a favour to John Gotti. But then Gravano got into the nitty gritty of exactly what it was the mob wanted to gain from the fight, and just how deep their influence on the sport would go. "My idea all along was to use the Snipes and Demioni fight as a set up to get Demioni a big pay-day against Mike Tyson. My plan was for Snipes to have a high ranking to make it look good, but to lose to Demioni... I'm sure we would have had no problem convincing Snipes to lose," he said.

Placing his glasses on and off his face, Gravano read his testimony clearly and distinctly to the watching Senators, which left them worried about the influence of organised crime in boxing. "Lots of people think organised crime makes its money from fixing fights and betting on the winner," he explained. "That doesn't happen any more. The 'purses' are so big it doesn't make sense to fix a fight in order to collect a bet. But we would consider fixing a fight for a bit of a pay-day from the money in the purses." He said the 'Family' plan was to "get a piece" of a successful boxer. "Until a boxer reaches a certain level there is not much money to be made, because the purse is small. Once they become successful, the Family can profit from that success. Now, because the size of the purse has gotten so big over the past 20 years, organised crime is more interested in getting back into it."

Under questioning, Gravano said that the mob lost interest in boxing in the 1960s when they became more sophisticated and got involved in construction, clothing, garbage and shipping. But, he said, in the late 1980s they had again turned to the sport as a way of making big money. "We got back into boxing over a period of time and recently we have had an interest. John (Gotti) had urged me to reach out… There is a lot of different benefits from it. At one point I myself negotiated to buy Gleason's Gym, as it had name and reputation," he said, and then described the money laundering opportunities available within boxing for a criminal organisation. We would probably start off with getting a gym, we'd have some trainers to train there. If the purses became big and lucrative when you get into 500k and better we would be able to chew up some of the money within the gym through training expenses… people being put to work in the boxer's corner… through promotional… for many reasons."

Gravano detailed how the Family hoped that they could make useful connections with wealthy business people through their role in boxing – naming Steve Wynn and Donald Trump as just two. "Our eyes wouldn't stop at boxing in these circles. If I was able to start we would have put a 'Captain' from our family in charge of the boxing industry, and once we had a good hold on it we would have branched off in as many areas as we could have," he said. Snipes was at his lowest ebb when he was earmarked by the mob and, according to Gravano, would have been grateful for a fight, but outside forces intervened and the Mafia plans were parked.

Despite the revealing testimony of the mafiosa turncoat, it seemed hard to believe that in the modern world it was still acceptable to have commercial sport and an international drug cartel hand in hand.

I wondered whether I was jumping to conclusions and were the links between MGM and the Irish mafia really as black and white as they appeared to me? At the same time, the violence of the drug world that the Kinahans inhabited was all too real in Dublin, when three women were shot in the legs while smoking outside a pub at a 21st birthday celebration. A gunman, there to kill Greg Lynch, the mob's man from Oliver Bond, also botched the hit and left the drug dealer horrifically injured after shooting him in the face.

In the days before his fight we found a picture of Macklin posing with Daniel Kinahan and Gary Hutch at a dinner party hosted by the Irish mafia in his honour. It was taken at their home, just a few nights before he flew to the US. The pair had been forced to host the farewell bash for Macklin because neither could travel to America due to the ongoing Operation Shovel investigations. On his Twitter account @djk236 even joked to friends that he had passport issues and couldn't make the fight. That was one way of putting it. But the truth was the US authorities had been alerted that Macklin could be travelling with criminals and those facing serious charges, and were on the lookout for a number of those who were expected to fly – including Kinahan. At the last minute, Nelson hurt his shoulder and Lamar Russ stepped into the ring at the Boardwalk Hall. The night was a triumph, and Macklin won on points, which was a cause for huge celebrations back in Spain.

A New Year rang in with new beginnings, as MGM signed boxer Anthony Fitzpatrick from The Monk's Corinthians Club. He joined a fast-growing number of boxing hopefuls from Dublin and Spain who were by then regulars at the gym and spending increasing periods of time on the Costa. Known as the 'Pride of Dublin', he was from the heart of the north inner-city and a close friend of Patsy Hutch, The Monk's brother.

Two months later, coach Danny Vaughan became part of the team. "We are growing all the time and this is a massive step in the right direction," MGM announced. Vaughan was fresh out of prison, after he had been nabbed with an ex-girlfriend for benefit fraud. The pair, Vaughan and Natalie Dickman, had scammed nearly £100,000 in 13 years, during which she pretended to be a single mum while he claimed to be her landlord, so they could claim social welfare. In reality the duo were a couple for years, had four children together and were living in his Liverpool home. The scam had started in 1996 and continued until 2009 when officials finally noticed. They had both pleaded guilty to two counts of obtaining services by deception and got 10 months in jail. During the sentence hearing, Vaughan's lawyers told the court that he took full responsibility for the scam, but was training seven boxers who were all possible champions.

When Peter McDonagh was signed to MGM in March 2014 he quipped: "Off to @MGM_Marbella where dreams become real." The boxer, a close friend of cricketer Darren Gough, had a troubled past, and as a child had moved from the Irish-speaking Connemara Gaeltacht in the west of Ireland, to Bermondsey in London, where his mother quickly abandoned the family. He joined a local boxing club and dreamed of becoming a champion, but in his early 20s he was charged with attempted murder and locked up for 23 hours a day in tough Belmarsh prison, as he awaited trial. Found not guilty, he returned to Ireland, but hit the drink and went through a dark period of his life before returning to England and rebooting his career.

Weeks after McDonagh's arrival on the Costa, MGM signed British Olympian Thomas Stalker, whose announcement that he was leaving Liverpool to train under Seamus Macklin, Matthew's brother, made front-page news. In an interview, Stalker said the chance to move his family to Spain was an "amazing opportunity" that he couldn't turn down. Up and coming in the ring, he had just won his seventh fight as a professional, and described MGM as "a world renowned" facility. In an interview with the *Liverpool Echo* he said: "After talks with my new manager, Daniel Kinahan, and trainer Seamus, we have created a plan for a new boxing journey together. This opportunity felt right at this stage of my career."

The sentence seemed to go unnoticed and unchallenged, the name slipping into the celebration of Stalker's new career like any other legitimate part of the team.

Quickly Declan Geraghty was signed and the young boxer from Dublin was also to be managed by Kinahan. When boxing trainer Johnney Roye posted a picture of a stunning mansion, complete with swimming pool, as his home-from-home while working for MGM, he also thanked both the gym and Daniel personally for his luxury digs.

Reams of coverage and interviews with boxers linked to the club were being featured on iFL TV – a YouTube channel which had been started by boxing fanatic Kugan Cassius. Cassius had worked as a bodyguard for British boxing legend Ricky 'The Hitman' Hatton, a close friend of Macklin. For years he had been going behind the scenes at boxing events with his camera and microphone. While he had managed to secure a decent online following, like many new media entrepreneurs he'd struggled to finance his venture and pay his bills. By the summer of 2014, Cassius was thinking of folding the station, as he couldn't work for free any longer. But a sponsorship deal from MGM meant iFL TV could be kept afloat and would get special access to all the gym's boxers, coaches and events. For Cassius it was a lifeline, but for Kinahan and Macklin it was a no-brainer when it came to publicity and marketing.

As the links between Macklin, his boxers and the mob were becoming more and more evident, it seemed that Kinahan was taking his new-found interest in marketing into his criminal career, too, and if anyone needed a reminder of how powerful the Irish mafia had become it was to be displayed in amazing technicolour back home.

The Kinahan brothers had returned to Dublin on a number of occasions during 2014, as their mother moved home to die after a diagnosis of terminal cancer. The return of her sons to the Oliver Bond flats complex in May for her funeral was planned with precision, just like a scene from a Godfather movie. While locals rallied with sandwiches and words of comfort, the old flat complex was put into lockdown, with an army of spotters and enforcers sent out to patrol the area like a militia.

Our own photographers who were there on the day were warned to leave "or else". Without any police back-up and with just a camera for protection, they would have been forgiven if they headed for the hills, but they stayed to record the scenes.

The youngsters marched up and down John's Lane Church and around the nearby Augustinian Church, as a stream of black stretched limos brought the brothers and their designer clad entourage to the church. There were bodyguards, out-riders and perfectly preened women at their side, as they took on the guise of rich businessmen.

Despite the outpouring of grief, it had not gone unnoticed by mourners that strange graffiti had been painted on the walls of a nearby Russian Orthodox Church. The slogans, snapped by the photographers, read: "Gary Hutch U Rat. The 'Rat'."

After the funeral, all eyes were back on boxing. Flying high on his own reignited career, Macklin had started talking about a long-awaited homecoming to Dublin for a showdown with Limerick boxer Andy Lee. Eventually, the announcement was made that he would headline a fight on August 30th.

"5 years since I boxed in Ireland and 4 years since I boxed in UK," Macklin tweeted. "Nice to be fighting back over this side of the Atlantic!"

Eddie Hearn of Matchroom Boxing, it was reported, had visited Macklin in his gym to seal the deal. If ever MGM was to place itself on the international boxing map, this was it.

But, it seemed, there had been other deals reneged upon in

a world of very different rules, where a bullet in the head is just another way of doing business.

Behind the scenes, Gary Hutch was getting increasingly irritated over money. In February 2009 he'd been part of a gang that had conducted a daring tiger robbery which had netted them an enormous €7.5 million from the Bank of Ireland on College Green. Some of the money was later recovered, but Gary, arrested and released without charge, had invested his share into the 'mob' through Daniel Kinahan.

Operation Shovel had followed and despite constant promises from Kinahan that his investment would be replenished with time, it never had been. Four years on, tensions were rising and he was getting frustrated with the constant excuses, while the Byrnes and their overlord, Bomber Kavanagh, took gangster bling to a new level.

Often, Bomber would return for visits to Crumlin laden down with gifts of jewellery and furs. When his wife, Joanne, turned 40, he splashed out more than €100,000 so she could celebrate her party with some gal pals who had been flown all-expenses-paid to Las Vegas for the holiday of a lifetime. The group of 23 had stayed at the Wynn hotel where rooms cost more than €20,000, and while there they had gorged themselves at roulette tables, restaurants and shopped at the resort's luxury outlets including Chanel, Christian Dior, Cartier, Louis Vuitton and Hermes.

The Byrnes had also travelled en masse to Mexico, where they had booked out one of the most expensive hotels in Cancun, and the family had snapped up villas in Majorca and properties on Ibiza. They were seen at Aintree and Ascot dressed to the nines and seated within the VIP enclosures exclusively used by owners and trainers. Social media postings showed one holiday after the other in the sun, complete with private villas, days on yachts and frolics on jet skis.

While Gary Hutch was looking with envy at the spending of the Byrnes, I was watching, too, but for totally different reasons. In my world they had become Ireland's first family of crime.

Dublin is a small city, with a population of just 1.2 million and gangland is even smaller, with key members of mobs often related or inter-married. For decades gardai had tried to break through the walls around the Byrne mob, but had found that blood ties had made their task virtually impossible.

The group had originally formed around the Roe family – a street-trading clan who hailed from Dublin's Liberties. Ambitious Sadie Roe became the central fulcrum of the wider family group when she married fraudster 'Jaws' Byrne, creating the perfect storm for a business which would be passed on through the generations.

The couple had two children, nine months apart, in 1973, James Jnr and Joanne, followed by Melanie a year later and Maria in 1978. Liam was born in 1980 while David was the youngest, born in 1982. Growing up, Sadie and her sister Christine, the mother of 'Fat' Freddie Thompson, were inseparable, but while one was happy with her spot selling flowers on Grafton Street, the other believed it was beneath her.

Sadie loved a fur coat and gold jewellery, which she believed set her above her contemporaries in the flats. When she and Jaws bought their home, 18 Raleigh Square, Crumlin, when their children were young, they vowed their step up in life was just the beginning. The house, a 1930s redbrick, was on a corner site and despite the fact that the couple left the original owners' name on the Land Registry documents, it was Jaws who eventually listed himself as owner in 1999, and in 2004 he applied to build another property in the large site at the back.

The Byrne family kept a tight inner circle and over the years created a fortress around the family home, buying up numerous properties that formed a circle around number 18. When Jaws eventually got planning permission and built a small bungalow in the side garden, his daughter Maria moved in. The recipient of a large compensation claim after a car accident, she would be later listed as the owner of her brother Liam's property, around the corner at number 2, and her brother David's property, directly across the road at 213 Kildare Road.

While Jaws had made his money through forgery and old-school crime, his off-spring were still only teenagers when they became heavily involved in drug dealing.

Sadie's siblings had provided them with plenty of back-up. Her sister, Collette, was the mother of notorious criminal Eoin 'Scarface' O'Connor, who survived a murder attempt in 2008. Christina had reared 'Fat' Freddie and his brother Richie, while Therese had borne a son, Liam Brannigan, who was also a key figure in the gang. Liam Roe, the son of Sadie's brother, James, also lived nearby and added his pumped-up muscle to the family business.

As they grew into adults the gang married their childhood sweethearts or the sisters of key associates. When the Crumlin and Drimnagh feud got underway for the drug territory they worked, 'Fat' Freddie took on the role as chief defender against rival Brian Rattigan, while Liam took over the day-to-day running of their drug operation.

Liam could be very violent, and in 2002 he was jailed for four years for a savage assault on former League of Ireland soccer player Trevor Donnelly outside a takeaway, during which he had repeatedly hit him over the head with a baseball bat and threatened to shoot him. In the run -up to the court case, Donnelly and his girlfriend were threatened to such an extent they were put under police protection.

Sean McGovern had no blood ties to the Byrnes but he was accepted into the bosom of the family as Liam's best friend and business partner in the Active Car Sales company, set up in 2013 as a front for the growing cocaine mob.

Liam liked to live clean and rarely touched drink or drugs but was known for his short temper and his weakness for women. David, the youngest, was Sadie's favourite and loved to dress in white and drive fast cars. He was regarded as Liam's right-hand man within the group structure, although he liked to see himself as his equal.

Bomber was so high on the garda radar that he was one of the first targets of the newly-established CAB when it was formed in 1996 and they went after his Drimnagh home. By the time the house at Knocknaree Avenue came on the market with a guide price of €180,000, Joanne and Bomber were gone to Birmingham and out of reach of the Irish garda. Public records showed that they set up a car business there, TK Motors in 2010, and that they had bought a house, but the recession, cuts in the garda's policing budget, a public sector recruitment moratorium and a slump in morale all went in favour of the gang. As the numbers of garda fell each year from a high of more than 14,500 in 2009 to a low of just over 12,800 in 2015, the Byrnes and Bomber Kavanagh thrived.

At the same time, the Criminal Assets Bureau seemed to fall off the radar and while still working behind the scenes, totally lost its public profile as the tough policing force against organised crime. For years criminals had run scared of the CAB and had been forced to hide their wealth off shore or risk having it taken from them. But for a protracted period the Bureau went quiet, giving the likes of the Byrnes confidence to show off their wares, which they did full throttle. Sources told me that Bomber was running millions of euros of Kinahan drugs and weapons into Ireland and laundering money through his motor firm, and that he was the most significant figure in organised crime next to Daniel Kinahan. "Bomber is the main man, he is the number one," my contacts told me. "But be careful. He is as dangerous as you can get."

I arrived in Tamworth on a bright spring day not really sure what I would find but was immediately struck by the wealth and prosperity of the town. About a 20-minute drive from the centre of Birmingham, it is a pleasant mix of rural and urban, complete with a scattering of chic eateries and pubs along the main Peel Street. A hub of the motor industry for decades, one of the town's claims to fame is that it was the home of the Reliant motor company which made three-wheeled cars just like Derek 'Del Boy' Trotter's in the hit series Only Fools and Horses. By the time Bomber Kavanagh opened his own motor firm, Reliant was well gone, a victim of recessions and the demise of the British car industry.

I followed the directions to TK Motors and the addresses listed with Companies House in the UK, but unlike the other car sales businesses in the area there was no forecourt and after much ado, I had settled on the fact that it seemed to be made up of an address in an office building and no more.

When Kavanagh had sold his first house at Whitesands Road he had bought on the more expensive Sutton Road, which led directly into the centre of Tamworth. "He must have known we were coming," I joked to the photographers, as we drove up and down Sutton Road realising we could get no visual on the house whatsoever. If Bomber had chosen wisely, I had no doubt it had nothing to do with an insignificant little news team, but more that he could see anyone else that may be interested in watching him.

More often than not, our surveillance work took us to smaller targets than Bomber, ones that wouldn't be quite as aware that somebody might be watching through the blackened windows of a parked car, or from a nearby building. The lowest possible rung on the ladder were the street dealers, often users themselves who would hardly notice if there was a camera in their faces. But the higher we went, the more aware the subject was and there had been many times that I had purposely stepped into view for fear our cars were being mistaken for something far more sinister than a newspaper team.

Bomber's home was a mansion fit for a Premiership footballer and it stood large and elegant in its own grounds, fronted with landscaped gardens and a sweeping driveway behind electric gates. A huge green stretched out the back where I had been told a private bar and hot tub area had been installed for parties. Unfortunately, the house was on a very awkward corner of the road, facing onto fields and with absolutely nowhere to stop outside without standing out like a sore thumb. We managed to find the best spot we could and hoped that Bomber would come out before a nosy neighbour or the traffic police moved us on.

We watched as a gardener tended to the manicured lawns and planters. An old web page told me the house was a six-bedroomed home, complete with en-suite bathrooms and luxury living quarters. A gleaming white Range Rover sport sat in the drive along with a brand-new black Mercedes A Class. It was clear that neighbours in the affluent suburb must have thought that Bomber had the Midas touch when it came to car sales. I guessed they probably knew him as 'Thomas' rather than his tough street name.

Early one morning, we watched key associates of Kavanagh's from Ireland arrive at the house in taxis. They looked like they were coming from the airport with overnight bags. Shortly after their arrival, they were driven away. We followed as they made their way to a massive industrial estate, where a huge car auction was due to be held. Rows and rows of top-of-the-range motors, including Porsche and Range Rover were sold throughout the day. Later, back at the house, we watched as 10 top-end cars were unloaded into the driveway, then collected again for transport.

Throughout the week we watched as staff came and went from their home and even reversed the cars around, so they were facing the electric gates for whenever Bomber or Joanne went out. In the flesh, Bomber wore a resting thunderous face and never seemed to smile. On regular shopping trips to Birmingham he would sit in the passenger seat, watching the road and the mirrors while Joanne did the driving. The couple would return hours later laden down with bags of designer clothes. On other occasions, Bomber would have a driver who often sped away on a network of motorways and out of our vision at breakneck speed.

I never dared approach Bomber, as I suspected any stupid journalistic bravery could put us all in danger, and so our only chance at photographing him came during a daring manoeuvre in a car, one day, which we all would prefer to forget. I, to my shame, was driving.

Back in Dublin the Byrnes were even more blatant about their wealth, and had given us plenty of opportunities to see what they were worth both in their own postings on social media and through lavish public displays.

When Lee Byrne, Liam's eldest son, had graduated from school he was ferried around Crumlin in a soft top white Rolls-Royce. I had only ever seen one of those cars before in Monaco on the south coast of France and it looked oddly out of place in the working-class suburb. At number 2 Raleigh Square, Liam had embarked on some major home improvements, extending his house to twice its size. Aerial photographs showed that he had built a playground on the roof of a massive extension, which took up the entire garden and dwarfed the neighbouring properties. A few doors up, a similar renovation job was underway on an unoccupied property. At David's, too, and his pal Sean McGovern's property nearby, hundreds of thousands in improvements had transformed their ordinary homes into grotesque monuments of drug money.

Young associates of the group seemed confident, too, to flaunt their own wealth with Instagram and Facebook postings of Rolex watches won in bets, and collections of shoes and designer hats and gym wear that could have filled the rails at Harrods. One week the Byrne brothers, David and Liam, would be driving around the city centre, parking illegally off Grafton Street in a Range Rover Autobiography, a motor worth up to €150,000.

The next week we'd spot them in a Mercedes G Wagon, valued around €120,000 or even in a brand-new Rolls-Royce, Bentley or Ferrari. They were partying with UFC champ Conor McGregor, holidaying in yachts and booking out some of the most expensive hotels in Dublin for family celebrations. Among those regularly in their company was the millionaire caravan park owner, Maurice Sines, from the UK. So close was he to Bomber and the Byrne clan that he had even attended the christening of Liam's youngest child and provided the luxury transport for the occasion.

They had a confidence to them that was outside anything I had seen before in Ireland. On one occasion we were trying to photograph them near their homes and I was driving the surveillance Jeep, with a photographer crouching in the back behind blacked-out windows.

I watched as Jaws Byrne drove off in a Lexus Jeep and I followed a distance behind, until I saw him pull in at a garda checkpoint. I had edged up a bit towards him, hoping that he might have to get out of the car, but with that I'd heard screeching and to my right saw a silver BMW coming toward me at breakneck speed.

It was being driven by Sean McGovern – and David Byrne was standing up in the passenger seat, his head out the window, roaring as the car persisted towards me. He was dressed from head to toe in white.

My jaw hung in shock as the world started to move in slow

motion. I remember clicking my seat belt and beginning to move across the front of the car, clearly reasoning that the impact might only break my legs and not kill me.

In the back, the photographer was a sitting duck and I had been rendered speechless, unable to utter any warning. At the very last minute they swerved and drove off down the canal, all just yards from the garda checkpoint.

7

Trouble in Paradise

Coach Jamie Moore punched the code into the black metal door of the plush Spanish villa that Gary Hutch and Daniel Kinahan shared just outside Puerto Banus. The stunning property stood among manicured gardens, where the scent of jasmine filled the air. It had been a long night and he hadn't intended staying out until the early hours of the morning. But such was the way with a knees-up in the Costa's party town and it was often hard to keep track of time in the playground of the rich and famous.

Moore had loved MGM from the moment he set foot inside the gym and it wasn't just the fact that it was fitted out with the best equipment, air-conditioning and top-of-the-range fitness features, it was also because of the atmosphere which was all centred on camaraderie, success and encouragement. Local kids came in their droves for free training sessions with the older boxers and coaches and regular fundraisers helped raise money for 'Aspandem', a charity supporting children with disabilities.

After training and fitness classes, Moore and others regularly gathered upstairs at the 'Slainte' bar for a meal, or simply to sit around for hours discussing techniques and regimes. For boxers it was nirvana and everyone seemed to be able to just immerse themselves in it totally, while all the mundane stuff like paying the bills was looked after by administrative staff.

Even the location of MGM seemed to be heaven sent. Across the busy roundabout which led traffic into the pricey marina area of Puerto Banus was the famed La Sala restaurant, where many retired for a long lunch to escape the midday sun. Beside it was the popular Aqua Mist nightclub, which had also been the subject of much chat in the gym. Moore and Macklin weren't that bothered with going out and were intent on building up for his August 30th clash in Dublin's National Stadium, the world title eliminator, and a bout which was sure to put the boxer firmly back on the international map. But before that happened, Macklin was to take a starring role in the then annual charity extravaganza, which was gearing up to be the talk of the Marbella society set. The star-studded white collar night at the luxury H2O hotel was booked out, and it was hoped that the club could top the £68,000 raised the previous year. MGM and its stable of boxers and trainers already enjoyed a certain celebrity around the Costa and were regularly asked to pose for photographs with tourists. Moore often had to pinch himself when he realised he was now part of it all.

There was no doubt that Macklin and Moore were unlikely friends who had found one another in the heat of a battle so brutal, that it was still the stuff of legend in the boxing world.

Eight years previously, the duo had fought for the British light-middleweight title over 10 rounds of gruelling sportsmanship that had never since been rivalled. It was in the 10th round that Moore had eventually overcome the 'Tipperary Tornado' in a knockout blow that was both thrilling and terrifying in equal measure.

Despite winning the fight, Moore had watched in horror as Macklin fell, looking gravely hurt. He had been so delighted to see the boxer breathe again and then speak, that he bent down to kiss him and later visited the hospital where he was recovering. Their friendship that followed had been far more special than the win, and had been born from two warriors who had brought one another to the brink of death. Moore had been in Macklin's corner ever since, and moving to Spain as his coach had cemented their brotherly bond.

It was difficult to stay away from the lure of Puerto Banus but Macklin was serious about his sport. Daniel Kinahan, too, was a sporadic socialite and his healthy eating, healthy living lead kept a lot of the lads in check. But he did call a session once every six weeks or so.

For Moore, the real 'Dan Kinahan' was at odds with his reputation. He may have been the son of infamous crime lord 'The Dapper Don' but all the boxer would later claim he knew of him was as a hard-working gym boss. As far as Moore was concerned, Kinahan had no convictions and looked after the MGM lads as they trained at the gym. In return, they were expected to be loyal and to give it their all – and were often seen on sunrise runs in the mountains or at weight training sessions on the long white sands of Puerto Banus' three beaches.

That said, when they did go out they certainly knew how to party, and that particular night had been one hell of a blast.

Moore knew he would feel a sore head in the morning, as he fumbled at the gate with the security code. Daniel and Gary Hutch were asleep inside, having both cleared out from the party earlier in the night saying they were tired. Moore heard the click of the gate and pulled it open at the exact same time he made the decision in his head that this would be his last evening on the tiles before he and Macklin headed to Dublin.

The boxer stepped onto the driveway and listened for a second, as the gates closed firmly behind him and the electric hum gave way to the sound of the crickets clicking their heels in the warm night. There was no doubt that the villa was a palace and one of the most beautiful properties he had ever stayed in. The personal chef Gary and Daniel had hired to cook their meals was an added bonus. The villa, which was in a posh residential area between Marbella and Estepona, was near to Puerto Banus and was a regular hangout for some of the lads from the gym and many of their friends who came to visit from the UK or Ireland for a holiday in the sun. It had been the scene of all sorts of pranks in the past and the boxers loved nothing more than a laddish joke.

Moore made his way up the driveway as he heard the dull noise of the swimming pool filter in the distance. Suddenly he saw a figure in the darkness, standing in silence. He squinted and noticed that the man, dressed in black, had a ghoulish rubber Frankenstein mask on. "What the...?" he spluttered, not knowing what to do.

The gun looked like a toy, but it was pointing at him. If this was a joke Moore didn't find it amusing. He began to walk towards the door. "You know what? That's not even funny," he said to the shape. In an instant, the still night was shattered with the noise of a loud bang – and Moore felt a searing pain in his right hip. He fell to the ground, unsure what was happening. More bullets came. There was a second dart through his leg. This time the pain appeared to go right through and explode out the other side. His body went into shock and he began to shake violently. Then he heard a car drive off and he was left alone in the darkness.

Moore writhed in agony, but somehow his brain clicked into fight mode. He remembered his almighty battle with Macklin that had taken both mind and fists. Years in the ring had taught him one thing, never give up until the final bell. Clutching his leg he felt a warm, sticky puddle gather around him and realised he was losing blood fast. He knew he had been shot, the who and why would have to wait. He strained his head towards the villa and tried to call out, but there were no lights on and he wasn't sure he was even making a proper sound, despite the fact that the effort was sapping what energy he had left. All alone he knew he urgently needed medical assistance and didn't have the time to wait for someone to stumble upon him. He also knew that if he tried to stand up he could easily bleed to death.

He thought of Salford and the feel of the rain and of his wife Colleen who, seven months pregnant that night of the Macklin fight, had got up and left the stadium, too afraid to watch. He remembered how she had kept him awake later that night, afraid of concussion and letting him sleep. He wanted to see his children again. He wanted to live.

Painfully, he reached into his pocket for his mobile phone praying that there was enough charge on it, so he could use it to call for help. He punched in the digits 911and got an operator on the other end of the phone. She was Spanish, but was able to communicate in English with him as he told her he had been shot and was lying in the darkness on his own. Despite spending much time at the villa he had no idea of the address. He would later recount the events of that night in an interview with *The Guardian*, saying: "I could have easily panicked and stood up and I would have bled even more then. But I reached for my phone and got lucky. My phone usually goes dead every time I'm on a night out. But that afternoon I was a little tired and I knew I was in for a late night. So I had a sleep and put my phone on charge. That saved my life, because I could dial 911. I had no idea what was the right Spanish number but, apparently, no matter where you are, if you dial an emergency number it works."

Over the next 25 minutes, Moore drifted in and out of consciousness until eventually an ambulance traced his whereabouts from the signal on his phone. He was rushed to a local hospital where he underwent emergency surgery to remove one of the bullets which had narrowly missed an artery in his leg. He was very lucky to have lived.

Days later, from his hospital bed and following the surgery on his leg, Moore tweeted: "Thanks for all the well wishes. Overwhelmed, gutted and confused about what happened, but thank God I'm Ok. X." He later added: "It's at times like this that you realise how well your[sic] thought of. I've had unbelievable support. Means a lot it really does. #Boxing Family."

While Moore was confused about what had happened, Marbella police were sure that the shooting was not meant for the innocent sport star and had nothing to do with boxing. Instead, the Guardia Civil worried that it was a failed attack meant for Gary Hutch or Daniel Kinahan. The 'Paddies', as they were known, were unique. Never before had Spanish police known an Irish gang to hold such status on the Costa.

Cops knew that while Operation Shovel had been set up to dismantle the empire, the Irish had taken advantage of the country's grindingly slow justice system, and their high-powered lawyers had tied the magistrates in knots. In the years since, they had undoubtedly risen again – and intelligence was beginning to suggest that Daniel Kinahan, the son and heir to the throne, had been wielding his power more and more while his father was spending extensive periods in the Middle East, where it looked like he was feathering a nest for his retirement.

Rumours of disquiet between the Irish and some Russian and Ukrainian gangsters filtered back to the Guardia Civil through a network of notoriously dodgy informants. But in the absence of any other theory, a row over money was as good as any as an official line of enquiry.

Alongside the official police investigations, an underworld probe had also quickly got underway, ordered by Daniel Kinayhan and mob detectives. But it had come to a different conclusion about the security breach at the property. Word quickly filtered back to Dublin. Instead of looking to the Russians or Ukrainians, it seemed that within camp Kinahan the finger of blame was turning inwards and to a young associate of Gary Hutch, who had been partying with the group that night.

Just years previously it would have been unthinkable that Daniel Kinahan would place suspicion anywhere near his right-hand man but rows about money had intensified between the pair and their friendship was on the rocks.

Hutch was no pushover and wore his name with pride. It had given him a confident swagger, first on the streets of north inner-city Dublin and later in Spain and the Netherlands, where he organised shipments for the mob and signed off wholesale deals with major UK and Irish buyers. In the days following the shooting the police pursued the Russian lead, while the mob's internal investigation firmly focused on the young Hutch associate whose behaviour had raised eyebrows amongst the revellers during the night out. Some witnesses claimed the youngster had enjoyed too much cocaine and had got "mouthy" before he was thrown out of the club and told to go home and sober up. Others said his behaviour looked staged – and a public spat with Hutch was akin to a rehearsal for an amateur dramatics production.

Somehow, it was claimed, he had borrowed a car and made his way to the villa where he knew Hutch and Kinahan would return after the knees-up. Hutch insisted he was not involved in any plot and that the shooting was, in fact, meant for him. He said that the youngster was acting alone, but Kinahan wasn't easily convinced.

As investigations continued, MGM cancelled the much-anticipated H2O event which had been sold out, and Macklin announced that he was pulling out of his boxing extravaganza at Dublin's National Stadium, as a mark of respect to his injured coach.

Back in the Irish capital, garda intelligence suggested intense talks were going on – and a deal was being hammered out between Hutch and Kinahan which involved, they believed, an apology for the shooting and agreement that a hard lesson needed to be learned.

The information proved good and on the evening of August
15th – 12 days after the Jamie Moore shooting – a car carrying
two men crashed into a barrier at the Mater Hospital in Dublin.
It was shortly after 7.15pm, and gardai would later identify a
seriously injured passenger as the same person believed to be
the masked figure with the gun in Spain who had shot and
injured Jamie Moore. He had been shot in both legs and
driven to the hospital for treatment by another man. Whilst
his injuries were horrific, they were not life threatening and
medics were confident that he would recover well after surgery.

Those who attended the scene found no bullet holes in the
car and with no co-operation from the victim or his accomplice,
officers had to conclude that a punishment shooting had
happened somewhere in the city.

Moore returned home to Manchester as soon as he was
able to fly and there, in the first week of September, welcomed
Guardian journalist Donald McRae into his home to discuss
what had surely been one of the most awful experiences of his
life.

Their interview would run in the newspaper just days after
an even more significant incident occurred back in Spain,
where an uneasy calm had hung over the Irish mobsters and
their boxer friends since the high-profile incident.

It had been a regular Saturday afternoon at Harmon's Bar in
Marbella, a popular haunt for Irish holidaymakers who flock to
the area in their droves on and off season. Those sipping pints
and chatting with friends had no idea what they were about
to witness and many would be left with the images planted in
their minds forever.

Gerard 'Hatchet' Kavanagh had strolled into the bar in the

early evening and met with another man. He had the look of a gangster – tanned, bulked up and with the obligatory huge Rolex watch on his arm, but in Marbella burly tough guys were ten a penny and nobody gave him a second look. 'Hatchet' was feeling pretty good. Just months previously he had been in his son Jamie's corner when he beat American Michael Clark at the House of Blues in Boston.

It was shortly after 4.30pm when he and the other man, an associate of Daniel Kinahan, took a seat on the outside terrace at Harmon's and ordered some soft drinks. CCTV footage would later show two men, dressed in tight clothing and with masks on their faces, make towards 'Hatchet'. The cameras record the frame second by second as he realises what is happening and pushes his seat away as the shots start coming. His companion flees out of sight, while a second camera records Hatchet bursting through the door of the pub, an assassin in hot pursuit firing all the time. Inside the bar, while customers sip on pints, he falls to the floor and the gunman stands over him pumping several more shots into his body.

The cool and calculated murder of Hatchet sent shockwaves through the criminal community, who knew that his was a large scalp to take. Back in Ireland, gardai were perplexed. Whoever killed him so publicly in the busy tourist venue had the potential to start a war on the Costa, as Hatchet was aligned to Kinahan's mob and a business partner of the powerful Bomber Kavanagh, who was so important he was considered number two in the vast Kinahan organisation. Not only was it daring but it also threw unwanted focus onto the Irish gangsters in Spain, and was immediately linked back to the shooting of Moore just weeks previously at Daniel Kinahan's house.

Days after Hatchet's fall, *The Guardian* published its interview with Moore, who told how he was recovering in the bosom of his family from his traumatic ordeal.

In the piece he recounted how he was shot in the darkness by the masked stranger, how he frantically sought help from emergency services as he fretted his phone battery would die and how he floated in and out of consciousness as he waited for help.

"It's all very blurry, but I remember them putting a drip inside me and it really hurt – much more than the bullets," he recalled about his arrival in hospital. "When I woke I felt delirious, seeing all these nurses, but I was happy too. 'Yes, I'm alive…'"

Quizzed about the possibility that Daniel Kinahan's links to organised crime may have been the reason for the shooting, he insisted: "I've known Daniel eight months and never seen any problems. I've just seen him in the gym working with the lads. He's a great bloke and I cannot see that being the case."

In Spain, police disagreed, and again were looking at the activities of the Irish mob as they launched an inquiry into the assassination of Hatchet. For a second time they suggested that Ukranian or Russian mobs could be linked to the shooting at Harmon's Bar. But back in Ireland, gardai were not convinced. The hitmen had ripped off their masks as they fled and later torched the black BMW X5 which they had used as a getaway vehicle. The forensic burning of cars near the scene of a murder was a well-worn method of the Kinahan mob itself, and had become synonymous with their kills. The timing of the murder – just six weeks since the shooting of Jamie Moore – was suspicious but there had been trouble brewing about drug debts in Dublin, and it was possible that Hatchet had got the blame.

Officers started to piece together his activities from the recent past to see if they could explain why he had met his end in such a violent way. They discovered there had been a row with a hapless dealer in Dublin, who had run into trouble after he was hit with a large bill from the Criminal Assets Bureau. He had been slow to pay for his product and Hatchet had been asked to return home to intervene in the debt on behalf of the Kinahan mob.

Hatchet returned empty-handed to Spain, but the dealer insisted he had paid a chunk of the money he owed in cash to him. A year previously there had been another intervention in money owed by gangster Christopher 'Git' Zambra, a ruthless dealer who had also run into problems with the CAB, who were in the process of seizing his house when he was murdered in May 2014. Zambra was a major league cocaine dealer with serious connections in Ireland and a close associate of a feared criminal known as 'Mr Big'. Zambra himself had been linked to at least five gangland murders and had stood trial, but been acquitted, for the assassination of 'Champagne' John Carroll in 2009. In turn, Carroll was a cousin of veteran George 'the Penguin' Mitchell – the international drug and weapon trafficker based between Malaga and Holland. The Penguin often did business with The Dapper and had enjoyed a good working relationship with him on the Costa. So, while unpaid debts undoubtedly led to gun murders in gangland, Hatchet was a big player and had the backing of the feared Bomber and the Kinahans. Gardai couldn't quite tally what had gone down, unless of course he had fallen foul of his own.

One way or another, Daniel Kinahan wanted it known that he was afraid and that his people were under threat from other criminals on the Costa. Days after Hatchet's murder he made a public announcement that he was living in fear and, in a statement from his lawyer, he said that he would be seeking police protection.

Still facing a money laundering trial as a result of Operation Shovel and forced to sign on every week at a court, his lawyer Javier Arias confirmed to journalists that he would be applying for protection for his client. While doing so, he rubbished reports that Hatchet had connections with the Kinahan family, insisting the Irish gangster had no 'personal or working relationship' with Daniel. The statement was ludicrous, as Jamie Kavanagh had just agreed to join MGM with Kinahan as his manager in the weeks before his father's murder, after being finally wooed from the US.

By the time Hatchet's body was returned to Dublin for burial, the deal with Jamie was off and if there was any doubt as to who was behind the murder, the funeral made it clear. No mob members attended. Instead, Greg Lynch, with horrific facial injuries from his own brush with death, carried his uncle's coffin, while his best pal Paul Rice read a eulogy, describing Hatchet as a 'Santa Claus' like character who always returned home laden down with gifts. Lynch hadn't been seen in public since the shooting which had left him maimed, but another Dublin criminal, Michael 'Mad Mickey' Devoy, had been shot dead in retaliation. Increasingly it was looking as if the wrong guy might have been blamed – and that Lynch could have been a victim of his own, too.

At the same time as Hatchet was being laid to rest, Gary

Hutch left the Costa and moved to Amsterdam, under renewed suspicion from Kinahan that he was involved in the shooting of Jamie Moore.

Days after he arrived in the Dutch capital, information filtered back to Ireland that he had been kidnapped but had managed to escape. Intelligence suggested that Hutch had been snatched on a street and bundled into a car by three mobsters, but as they drove through Amsterdam he managed to open the back passenger door and throw himself out of the moving vehicle before running for his life. He was pursued but managed to escape through an alleyway and had gone to ground. The tale was like a scene from the film *The Bourne Identity*, with Gary Hutch apparently taking on the role of the hunted Jason Bourne, played by Matt Damon.

As events in Spain and the Netherlands heated up, in Ireland the Hutch side were coming under pressure to hand over the runaway Gary, or see a €100,000 contract placed on his head. The knee-capping of his young associate was not enough, and the row had suddenly become very serious. Rumours suggested that the Byrne brothers were representing the Kinahan interests, and when The Monk's brother Eddie turned down the request to present Gary to the mob, his house was attacked and all the windows were smashed. He later received a phone call from an increasingly irate Kinahan representative saying that if he didn't give up Gary, not only would he be murdered, but that other members of his family would also be attacked.

The street chatter was jumpy and well established informants within the Kinahan and Hutch organisations were warning their handlers that a war was looming if it wasn't sorted quickly. As Jamie Moore recovered from his injuries and Gary

Hutch remained on the run in Amsterdam, the Hutch family called on their Godfather.

Retired from hands-on crime for years and largely based in Lanzarote, The Monk was a diplomat in the criminal underworld and ultimately a family man. At 52 he felt he had worked hard for a lot of things in life and a bit of peace was one of them. For years he had warned his brother, Patsy, to get his sons in order and steer them away from the Dapper Don and his two boys, a relationship he had vowed would end in nothing but trouble. But still Gary had got in deeper and deeper, bringing many of his counterparts from the north inner-city with him. Those who knew The Monk said he was annoyed and concerned in equal measure about events that were happening in his native Dublin, and which were dragging him back to his past. He particularly did not want to get brought into any drugs war. But, under much persuasion, he had agreed to try to talk to his nephew.

Despite the trouble, Macklin's Dublin homecoming was rescheduled to November and a full house turned out at the 3 Arena for the biggest boxing night in Dublin for years.

The Kinahans and their cronies turned out in force at the weigh-in at the City West Hotel complex. Daniel attended, but looked shifty and nervous and disappeared soon afterwards. But Christopher Jnr hung around and went for a private meal with David Byrne and his cousin Liam Roe, amongst others, at a restaurant nearby – a clear sign of just how cosy the two crews had got. On the night the pals arrived en-masse to the 3 Arena, amongst those spotted in the crowds were Finnegan and Lynch.

Anthony 'Pride of Dublin' Fitzgerald was first up and he

walked towards the ring with Daniel at his side. Positioned in prime front-row seats were 'Jaws' Byrne and his sons David and Liam. In their seats at the 3 Arena the Byrnes were feeling very confident and throughout the night, as Jamie Moore was interviewed regularly on Sky television, Jaws often popped up in the background smiling and laughing with his boys.

Moore was back on form and days beforehand he posted photographs of his injuries on his Twitter account. One picture clearly showed where one bullet entered his leg and exited in a 'Y' shaped wound on the other side, while the other showed where the second bullet entered up into his hip area. While they cheered their fighters, MGM suffered a crushing defeat with both Fitzpatrick and Macklin beaten, while Declan Geraghty was disqualified.

Macklin had been pitted against the Argentinian Jorge Sebastian Heiland in a fight dubbed 'Return of the Mack'. But despite his efforts, he fell in the 10th, crushing his dreams of another world title shot. As he slumped and the bell rang, Kinahan was one of the first in the ring to help him back to his feet, and walked out of the arena with his arm around his pal after the devastating loss.

"Maybe I'm getting old," quipped Macklin later.

Mixing in the crowd, undercover officers from the National Drug Unit spotted Gerry 'The Monk' Hutch sitting alone. Also seated solo was Paul Rice, who had carried his friend Hatchet's coffin just weeks previous. Intelligence later suggested that while the Kinahan crew spoke to neither Hutch nor Rice, they did meet about a joint venture with members of the Keane gang in Limerick. It was in order to back them as they made an attempt to take over the turf left behind by a battered Dundon mob, who had been brought down by massive garda attention. Despite the crushing defeats, the mob partied anyway as a show of strength and even booked out the Audi bar at the stadium.

*****

The Monk returned to Dublin on a wet, dull February day and made his way straight to the north inner-city and to the home of his brother Patsy. He had tried to keep his visit quiet but, as usual, his presence in the area had set tongues wagging and a media photographer was there to record the event. Minutes after he was seen, an even lesser-spotted Hutch appeared on the same street, clad in a navy blue raincoat and tracksuit. The pictures plopped into the inbox at the *Sunday World* newspaper and we immediately snapped them up as exclusives. What may have looked like a picture of any other inner-city lad to most, was a very significant development in an emerging gangland story that was becoming ever more intriguing and dangerous.

The fact that Gary Hutch was back in Dublin meant there had been developments, and when he spotted the snapper hiding in a parked car Gary grinned from ear to ear and took on the casual appearance of a returning soldier ready to be greeted by a rendition of 'tie a yellow ribbon'. The gossip machine in the north inner-city probably works better than most high-end communications networks and quickly the story of the peace deal got out.

The Monk, the story went, had met with the Dapper Don – and the Hutch family had handed over a sum of €100,000 or €200,000, depending on who told the story, to buy Gary out of the mob. Like most information from gangland, the truth was probably in there somewhere, but nonetheless it was universally accepted that Gary's return to Dublin meant he was out of the woods, and that The Monk had managed to cut some slack for his nephew.

One month later the sound of gunshots shattered a still mid-morning in the leafy suburb of middle-class Drumcondra in Dublin. Paul Kavanagh was just 27 and the younger brother of Hatchet, working as the Dublin partner in his operation with Bomber. This time there were no Russians to blame and immediately the Kinahan mob were linked to the shooting, with speculation growing that Paul and his late brother Hatchet must have pocketed money and unleashed the wrath of the mob on their greed.

Paul was the last surviving son of Mary Kavanagh and the partner of moll Gemma Roe, a pretty blonde who was once stopped carrying cash home from Spain. Notable in their absence at his funeral were Rice and Lynch, who had carried Hatchet's coffin just months previously. There was no suggestion that there had been a falling out within the group, more that the pair were scared there was a bullet waiting for them, and a funeral was an ideal chance for an opportunistic assassin.

Since he'd been snubbed at the boxing night, Rice was under no illusion. The writing was on the wall, and he and his family disappeared from their Tallaght home, while Lynch had been living like a hermit at his. But posting photographers on the funeral wasn't a waste, as there was one familiar face in the crowd that day. Conor McGregor, a good friend of Jamie and the Kavanagh family, attended to pay his respects.

Fr Sean McArdle told the congregation in Drimnagh: "Remember that violence is never against one person, it devastates a family and a community." Through tears, Jamie Kavanagh added: "We were inseparable."

8

Clash of the Clans

Two months after he buried his uncle, and six months after his father was murdered in a Marbella bar, Jamie Kavanagh signed a four-fight contract with MGM and a managerial deal with Daniel Kinahan.

It was agreed that the then 25-year-old would train in London with the duo Jimmy and Mark Tibbs, while spending some time in Marbella. "My girlfriend is pregnant," he said, explaining his decision to move to the UK after what must have been a hugely traumatic period of his life. I wasn't the only one flabbergasted and confused. The news caused chatter in many quarters, not least amidst those still trying to figure out what exactly was happening within the Irish mafia.

"It's all about the money," my contact told me. "Make no mistake about that. Money buys everything. It buys loyalty."

One way or another, Kinahan must have pleaded the case well to Kavanagh that he had nothing to do with either murders, and clearly the boxer had accepted his word.

"I have known Jamie and his family for a long time," Kinahan said in a statement that was completely at odds with the one he had released through a solicitor just months before, when he sought protection after the murder of Kavanagh.

"I've followed him closely over the years, watched him train and develop here in Spain and I've seen the sacrifices he has made traveling to America while spending time away from his family and girlfriend," Kinahan said of his newest signing. "I think he is a world-class fighter and I am delighted to have him on board."

MGM by now boasted a host of boxing stars. They included Belfast-born Jamie 'The Mexican' Conlan, the older brother of the more successful Michael, who was set to represent Ireland in the 2016 Olympics along with his pal Paddy Barnes. Conlan had insisted that he was at first hesitant about the move to Spain, but later told *Boxing Monthly* that when Daniel Kinahan rang him he couldn't refuse. Speaking about life in Puerto Banus he described how the boxers forged a bond like no other by training, living and even eating together.

Derry Mathews and Iain Butcher were also added to Kinahan's portfolio, which at that point included Stalker, Fitzgerald, Geraghty and Bradley Saunders. In his statement when signing up to wear the black and gold, Matthews had said: "This is a great opportunity. I will be managed by someone who I believe will be one of the best managers in the world in the next few years."

MGM began a major push into Scotland, staging its first boxing show in Glasgow in the Bellahouston Leisure Centre in the summer of 2015. Then more Irish boxers signed up, including 'Big Sexy' Sean Turner, David Maguire and Ciaran

Mullen amongst others. Lights Out At The Plaza, MGM Promotions' first show in Marbella, took place as autumn swept in, headlining Macklin.

"This is where the gym is and this is where Daniel and I decided we were going to manage fighters and promote shows, so it's fitting that I'm headlining the… first professional boxing show here."

Lights Out At The Plaza sold out in 48 hours, with a full house to watch the eight fights, each featuring an MGM fighter. The following night saw the annual white-collar charity fundraiser. The Monk's old pal, the former boxer turned compere Big Joe Egan, MC'd both nights, and during the weigh-in for the charity gig dubbed 'Intense Face Offs', he introduced the two team captains to a high octane crowd.

"Ladies and gentlemen, yiz are very welcome here today. We will have the weigh-in now with the blue team from Kevin and the red team from Daniel," he said, as armed robber Kevin Lynch and mob boss Daniel Kinahan took to the podium.

Sponsors proudly plastered across the backdrop included Linekers and TIBU nightspots, while the Aspandem charity was the benefactor. Daniel and Christopher Jnr, dressed in red T-shirts, shorts and runners, shifted from foot to foot looking awkward, while Lynch, in a blue shirt, took on a much more confident stance. One by one the teams were called up. Dean Masterson was first to take to the stage on Daniel's side. The Dubliner grinned and joked with his opponent as the crowd cheered them on. Next up in red was Lee Gibson, who would be later named in court by the Criminal Assets Bureau as a close associate of Liam Byrne.

As the rivals were brought together and the crowds cheered,

Kinahan constantly hopped around clapping the boxers on the back and shaking hands with those brought up to the face-off. Amongst the younger boxers were Kinahan's own son, Sean, and a young relative of Paul Rice. Finally, the captains of the teams were brought forward for a forehead to forehead push, as the crowd whooped and cheered.

Days later, four more boxers were added to the MGM stable. They all hailed from Liverpool and included Jazza Dickens and Kevin Satchell. In a statement the gym said: "MGM management and Frank Warren will help them on to world titles as soon as possible."

As the gym appeared to get more and more crowded, promoters and coaches from the boxing world looked on stunned at the amount of money there seemed to be to buy up the talent. British champion Billy Joe Saunders flew out with his trainer, Jimmy Tibbs, for a few weeks to use the facility and gushed that the climate, facilities and everything was "perfect". The lure of the MGM money would soon draw him, too, but as the gym gained more and more notoriety, another murder was set to be linked back to Kinahan and his operations on the Costa.

The shooting of Gary Hutch on a Thursday morning near Marbella went almost unnoticed by Spanish media, who had no understanding of the significance of it within the Irish mafia or indeed to the boxing giant of MGM. But those who understood the power of the Hutch and Kinahan sides knew one thing – it was war.

In Spain, the murder focused police attention firmly on the gym and some of its members, and also on the previous murder of 'Hatchet' in Marbella. It set in train a co-operative investigative partnership between Irish garda and the Spanish Guardia Civil that would prove hugely effective in fighting organised crime, and one that would set a blueprint for future enquiries into Irish mobs.

Nobody could quite work out why Hutch had returned to Spain. Contacts of mine said he had been convinced that the pay-off arranged by The Monk had put an end to any bad blood between himself and Daniel Kinahan and he felt comfortable to return to set himself up as an independent wholesaler.

"Whoever told him he'd be safe must have been pretty convincing, that's all I can say," one source said. "It was an absolutely mad thing to do. He walked right into the lions' den."

Patsy and Kay Hutch buried their son in his home of Dublin and pleaded at his funeral mass for no retaliation to be taken for his death. But for his associates, his murder was a call to war and no pleas from his grieving mother would be heard.

Two weeks later a jailhouse knife attack was attempted on his older brother 'Del Boy' on the back of a €10,000 bounty that prison authorities believed had originated in Spain. The attack appeared to be a warning from the Kinahan mob that they could get to 'Del Boy' and that those planning any revenge for Gary's murder should put the thought out of their head. But just as tensions were heightening in the capital, the entire Kinahan mob were planning a trip home.

In November, just two months after the murder of Hutch, MGM were back in Dublin at a 'Second Coming' event in the National Stadium, headlining Jamie Conlan with a host of boxers out in force and every seat full. Drama at the press conference ensured the headlines. Peter McDonagh's opponent accused him of not being Irish, while Sean Turner claimed he was in good shape because there was "no chipper or kebab shop" in Spain. Turner's pal, the Olympic hopeful Paddy Barnes, stepped in for a mock face-off when his opponent didn't show up.

For many, the highlight of the night was also Kavanagh's much-anticipated first fight in Ireland. Again, there was a big divide between news and sports reporting and the show was hailed a triumph for MGM given its short time in business. In post-fight interviews Macklin promised there would be regular shows in Dublin so that boxers could build up their fan base and get television exposure for their sport. Speaking about the work he had done to get the show on the road, he insisted that he wasn't the one to be thanked.

"To be honest, Daniel deserves most of the credit and also Anto as they're the ones who are really hands-on and deal with everything day to day. I give my opinion and advice but they're the lads that are making it happen."

But as boxing correspondents hailed the show a huge success and began to talk about hopes for another day out in the capital, the dark shadow of organised crime moved in over the festivities.

It was around lunchtime in the newsroom when the phone rang.

"Is that Nicola Tallant?" the voice asked. "There was an attempted shooting last night. At the Red Cow. You need to know this."

The Red Cow is a big hotel on the outskirts of the capital, famous as the stop-off point for people from the midlands, south and west of Ireland visiting Dublin. They descend on the Red Cow en-masse during Gaelic Season, on Black Friday and often for concerts and events like the garden show 'Bloom'. Located at the intersection of the N7 which travels from Dublin to Limerick and Cork and the M50, which circles the city, it is busy and popular with families as much as country music fans. It is not the sort of place I would have associated with a shooting.

"Excuse me?" I said. "Did you say a shooting?"

The caller was nervous but he continued. "It was a big boxing night. Liam Byrne was there. Liam Roe. Kinahan. They saw them... in the car park. With wigs and with the gun."

The man on the end of the phone certainly had my attention. It wasn't often that a ring-in on a Saturday would be so significant.

"They saw them and they all sped off. That's all I can say. It's bad. It's going to be bad."

With that my caller hung up and I sat for a moment with the receiver in my hand. If the information was right and there had been a shooting attempt on Byrne, Roe and particularly one of the Kinahan brothers, this was a serious escalation in tensions around the mob, and the first possible kickback since the murder of Gary Hutch.

I picked up my own phone and tried to establish what I could. I quickly discovered that an incident had indeed been reported to gardai but there was nobody at the hotel by the time they arrived. CCTV later confirmed that something had happened in the car park and that a Volvo had arrived and left without the occupants exiting the vehicle. Later, an abandoned car of a similar make had been found in the Ballyfermot area of the city, abandoned and burned out. It had been red in colour. Gardai had begun to hear a similar story to what I was piecing together. Liam Roe had possibly stepped outside for a cigarette at some point during a big knees-up and spotted two shadowy figures in a car outside. Some witnesses and grainy CCTV suggested that a gun, or something that could have been one, may have been produced, but that it didn't fire and the car suddenly sped off as panic ensued inside and revellers began to flee the building.

Later, I learned that Daniel Kinahan was inside and that he had fled to safety in a silver Mercedes G wagon, driven by David Byrne. The significance of the event and the possibility that an assassin had lain in wait outside was not to be underestimated, and I spent the afternoon ringing around contacts and trying to ascertain what exactly this could mean. The headline over my story the following morning said it all in two words: 'Hits War.' Inside the newspaper, I wrote extensively about the incident. "This is a clear message to the Kinahans: There will be blood," a source had told me.

My story was accompanied by a picture of Daniel Kinahan, taken by our photographer outside the five-star Westbury Hotel off Grafton Street, which we knew was his favourite place to stay whenever he was in town. I often found it extraordinary that we had photographed him and other members of his mob, whose lives were under threat, so frequently and so easily. We had no inside intelligence on where they would be, we just followed their habits and our gut instincts. Most of the time we got lucky, as they were largely creatures of habit despite all the expensive training they had in counter-surveillance techniques.

The incident had happened shortly after 9.30pm. According to my sources there were between 50 and 100 revellers inside celebrating the success of the 'Second Coming' event, when word got around that there was a gunman outside. One of the customers who had witnessed the mayhem had called the gardai. Years later it would be argued that Liam Roe had not been in attendance and that the gunman had gone for Daniel Kinahan and not him, but that original source of information was immediate and his story was backed up between the garda reports, the burned-out car and the CCTV at the hotel. Also, it would be hard to mistake Liam Roe for anyone else – he wasn't called Tango One for nothing. Roe was a big burly beefcake who was prone to taking tanning injections which had given his skin a bizarre orange tone. Of all the extended Byrne crew, he was unmistakable. Regularly, the photo editor at the time would call me from across the office and ask me if I could identify Roe from a group picture he had on his screen.

"I'm just not sure which one he is," he'd call over to me.

I would dutifully trudge across the newsroom willing to help only for our back bench of page designers to double over in tears of laughter. The picture on the screen would inevitably be of a group of faces with one tangerine one looking out. You could recognise Liam Roe from outer space.

The week after the botched attack at the Red Cow another army declared a different kind of war, when eight suicide bombers massacred 129 people in France – killing the majority in the Bataclan nightclub in Paris. Horrific scenes played out on grainy video footage taken by revellers, as party-goers and students were shot down in the prime of their lives. As the world united with France in grief and outrage, the brewing Kinahan and Hutch feud was briefly forgotten. But tensions wouldn't be quelled for long. It seemed revenge would be a dish best served cold and, as the MGM boxers once again headed for home turf, a plan was being put in place.

There was no doubt but the pictures were becoming boring, and for the news pages one boxing weigh-in looked just like the last. We had loads of them from MGM's previous events and I had seen Daniel Kinahan in a grey tracksuit more times than I cared to remember. None the less, tensions between the Kinahan and Hutch sides had been increasing since the Red Cow incident, and over the festive season there had been reports that The Monk had survived an assassination attempt in Lanzarote when his sixth sense told him to leave a pub where he was ringing in the New Year. While no shots had been fired, the pair – who Hutch recognised from the north inner-city – were on a mission to kill, although the Hutch camp denied the incident had happened at all and tried to quash the story.

Little had become clear since the murder of Gary Hutch other than the fact that both sides begged to differ about the deal done to spare his life and everything else that had happened since. And of course, when it came to sides, it was difficult to work out who was aligned to who. After all, the mob had once been a single gang and many rivals now appeared to be living in the same communities, which was a recipe for disaster.

One way or another it was quiet in news terms, so on the morning of February 5th 2016, it was felt that there was no harm having a look at the weigh-an event that was due to take place around lunchtime at the Regency Hotel near Dublin Airport.

MGM's Clash Of The Clans night was scheduled for the following evening at the National Stadium. Daniel Kinahan was expected as his new protégé, Jamie Kavanagh, was one of the stars of the show and there was every chance he'd be in attendance at the Regency, so a photographer and a journalist were dispatched for a day that would be implanted on Dublin for years to come. Jamie Conlan had been due to headline the event, but the Belfast man had to pull out in the run-up due to injury, leaving Jamie Kavanagh centre stage.

Kavanagh and Portuguese veteran Antonio Joao Bento would fight it out for the WBO European lightweight title, while Sean Turner and Paul Built were set to slug for the heavyweight category. Other MGM fighters, including Sean Creagh, Gary Sweeney and Declan Geraghty were also due to take to the ring on the night, which was set to be televised by BoxNation, a subscription-based channel linked to BT Sport. 'Pride of Dublin' Anthony Fitzgerald's name was there, too, on the undercard, despite the fact that he was still known to be very close to the Hutch family and had attended Gary Hutch's funeral just months previously.

The weigh-in got underway at 2pm, but our team stayed outside as the sporting side of the occasion was being well covered by boxing writers and we were really only interested to see who was there and who was with who.

In less than half an hour the fate of so many in that room and those linked to them changed forever. The call from the photographer was frantic, and the information sketchy. I could hear the panic playing out in the background.

There had been a shooting.

Someone was dead.

Our guys had got in the way of a getaway van, had a Kalashnikov pointed at them and felt very lucky to be alive. If that wasn't enough drama for one day, there was a picture taken as a guy with a gun ran to the getaway vehicle. The photographer had seen him while he was sat in our Jeep, wondering what had happened inside the Regency having heard gunshots. He'd raised his camera to his eye and pressed.

Click, click, click, click, click, click, click, click, click.

Nine times the camera lens shuttered.

As the hit team began their getaway, the photographer had dropped his gaze to the back of his camera and started to move through the frames. Just once he had captured a crystal clear image of what had been in front of him for just an instance. Once was enough.

The picture, which would later be seized by gardai under warrant, would become an iconic image of gangland crime in Ireland. It showed a man in a flat cap, gun in hand, running away from the Regency. To his right, a man in drag, also carrying a gun, used his free hand to start to remove the wig on his head. Dressed in boots, leggings and a knee-length coat, his lips a deep stain, his eyes made up and black glasses on his face. Chilling in its clarity, a moment captured in time that speaks volumes of the coldness of murder, it was to become one of the most controversial aspects of the boxing weigh-in – a sliding doors moment which would fuel conspiracies for years to come and which would cause a whole lot of trouble for a whole host of people.

As the day wore on, the events that had played out inside the Regency were slowly being pieced together. It seemed that the proceedings had got underway in the hotel function room as a silver Ford Transit Van had pulled up at the gate which separated the hotel from a housing estate next door. Captured on CCTV, a man in a wig and another wearing a flat cap were seen going in through the hotel's unlocked laundry entrance, sometime after 2.20pm. Inside, accountant Margaret Christie saw the peculiar-looking pair make their way through the hotel arm in arm. She would later recall how she knew that the woman in the blonde wig, black rimmed glasses, coat and knee-high brown boots was really a man, when she saw him going over on his ankle. "That's a man dressed up as a woman," she said laughing, and with that the wig slipped, she would later tell a court, and she saw his hair was jet black. She presumed it was a joke.

Inside the function room Gary Sweeney was on stage, dressed in a pair of superman underpants. Mel Christle, the then president of the Boxing Union of Ireland, scribbled down details as he stepped off the scales. Shaky video footage from a mobile phone, which would later be screened across the world, captured what happened next. There was a bang and then chaos. Seconds after the first gunshots were fired inside the function room the crowds started to run for their lives. Confused and terrified, some dived for cover while others swept children up in their arms. The sickening cracks filled the air. As the crowds lurched to the hotel reception, many would later describe an instant when they thought they were saved – when the familiarity of the garda uniform flooded them with relief.

"It's OK! It's the ERU!" someone called out, just as two more uniformed figures, helmeted and dressed in blue garda jackets, walked calmly into the ensuing panic.

But the mayhem and the horror was only beginning. The details were a little off – like the scarves over the men's faces, the ill-fitting uniform, the oversized guns – but it didn't register with the frightened crowd, who began to move toward them. Just as they did, one of them aimed his rifle and opened fire. They weren't gardai at all, but a second hit team there to finish off what had been started in the function room.

In the reception, a scene would later be described in detail by survivors. On the floor an injured man clutched himself in agony. The shooter stood calmly on the desk in the foyer, the AK47 assault rifle in one hand. Despite the hysterical screaming, many noted that his breath seemed to rise and lower steadily in his chest. He was calm. He turned and pointed his weapon at the man who was cowering behind the reception desk. The BBC sports journalist Kevin McAnena looked down the barrel of the gun and screamed: "Don't shoot. Don't shoot." He would later speculate that his accent had saved him – but the truth was that the shooter could never have mistaken him for Daniel Kinahan from such close range.

He knew Kinahan well and had once been one of his soldiers on the Spanish Costa.

The shooter never missed a beat.

He raised the weapon and fired at the injured man on the floor below him. David Byrne's body shook from the violence of the gunfire. He was definitely dead. The gunman jumped down onto the floor of the lobby, coldly walked passed the body of his victim and made his way to the waiting van.

He was joined by the other uniformed hitmen and then by the man in the flat cap holding a handgun in his right hand and the man in the knee-high boots and blonde wig. They began to run towards the van waiting outside.

And the camera had started to click. Sliding doors.

Outside the Regency, a crowd gathered in the car park.

Pictures would later show Liam Roe incandescent with rage, while Liam Byrne talked frantically on a mobile phone. Beside them, Sean McGovern clutched his injured leg which had been grazed by a flying bullet and Aaron Bulger, a young Tallaght man, lay on the ground as pals tended to his stomach wound. Bolger had been knocking around with the Kinahan crew for years and had been one of the youngsters we had identified in Puerto Banus in 2013.

Inside, on the floor, David Byrne lay in a pool of blood, his white runners stained red. There was no sign of Daniel Kinahan who'd been at the weigh-in, but who had escaped just before the gunfire started. Unlike the rest of the crowd who had surged towards the front doors and the waiting hitmen dressed as garda, he had fled out the back. Mayhem ensued even after the real garda had arrived and one witness spotted Jamie Kavanagh, vomiting against a wall, white with shock. Just a year since he had lost his father and months after his uncle's death, the horrors of gun violence had again visited his life in spectacular fashion.

At 5.53pm he tweeted: "Anyone asking I'm OK! Thank you for asking. I was lucky today is all I can say…"

While his body still lay contorted in the hotel reception, it was clear that David Byrne had not been the target, but had been killed when the assassins couldn't find Daniel Kinahan.

Gardai and reporters arrived at the scene en-masse as the significance of what had happened started to sink in. Some boxers hung around to give interviews, others fled. Butlin's promoter Carl Greaves told his local newspaper, *The Nottingham Post*, that he initially thought a fight had broken out in the crowd, but then realised there were guns.

CLASH OF THE CLANS

"It was bullets and everybody just ran. People ran for the front door. I just ran for the nearest exit. It was terrifying and all I could think about was my family. I just ran as fast as I could and just kept going. We bunkered down in a pub until it was safe to return. When we got back, there was a tent that had been put up where obviously there was somebody inside... At the time, your instincts take over, but the more and more I think about it, I am a lot worse now than I was earlier. I just want to get back to my family."

The dogs on the streets knew that the Regency was the work of the Hutch mob and while it was planned with precision, as only The Monk knew how, it had been a spectacular failure. While the public were shocked by such a bold display of violence, those of us who had even a small insight into matters of crime knew one thing – the attempt to cut off the head of the snake had been an unmitigated disaster and The Monk was in big trouble. In gangland terms he had put all his money on black but the pill had stopped on red.

Later, a few gathered in a pub in town and whispered the tit-bits of information that were coming through on the phones. McGovern was dead and alive a number of times over the course of the evening, but in the end we settled on the fact that he had checked himself out of a Dublin hospital and was quite well. Bolger had been admitted but was in fighting form and eventually posted a picture of himself on social media in his hospital bed, giving two fingers to the camera.

There was little word of the whereabouts of Daniel Kinahan, but we did get an inkling that there was a summit at Raleigh Square, where a distraught Sadie Byrne was spitting fire about her youngest son. This was no ordinary murder, that was clear from the very beginning, and while there was no doubt we had bagged a big gangland exclusive, I had a bad feeling that our presence at the scene was going to be misconstrued.

Saturdays are the busiest day in the *Sunday World* newsroom, but in my career there were few that could have been compared to February 6th 2016. With a general election just weeks away, politicians were out in force vowing to tackle organised crime, the garda were coming under huge criticism due to their lack of presence at the weigh-in event, but most importantly the threat of retaliation loomed like a dark cloud over Dublin. You could almost hear the thunder.

My phone pinged around mid-morning – a reminder to see if there was anyone free to go along to the National Stadium for the Clash Of The Clans event. In the office there was chaos. The photograph taken at the scene of the murder of David Byrne was sensational and the editors wanted to run it unpixelated, but the garda were threatening to go to the High Court to injunct the publication of the newspaper – which would have been a first in its 40-year-plus history. A stand-off had ensued until eventually an Assistant Commissioner arrived with a warrant to seize it and try to negotiate with the Editor, so relations could remain cordial.

It was agreed that the newspaper would publish the picture and be damned, albeit while blurring the faces of the two gunmen. At the same time, our journalists were desperately trying to identify flat cap and the man disguised as a woman.

In the north our best forager, who could always be relied upon to unearth the truth, was hard at work on the pavements. He had called up all his contacts and had eventually nominated a dissident Republican called Kevin Murray as the older man wearing the hat. Murray had life-long links to a variety of terror groups and was from Strabane in County Tyrone. At that point he was a member of 'RAAD' or the Republican Action Against Drugs group, which had been set up around six years earlier. With members often suspected of being radical former IRA and INLA volunteers, the group had been linked to a string of shootings and bomb attacks in the north – claiming to be against drug dealing. Like most of the dissident groups, the reality was far from an upstanding public service and RAAD had announced a merger in 2012 with the Real IRA. While only 47 years of age, Murray looked a lot older and appeared to be back in his home in Strabane, although unsurprisingly wasn't answering the door.

In Dublin the identification process was slower. While the man in drag was suspected of being "a Hutch" mobster, nobody was quite sure which one. The heavy make-up, wig and glasses made the identity difficult. We took solace from the fact that even if we had been able to run the snap without the pixelation, no one would have known who it was anyway.

At some point during the day my desk phone rang. There was a man on the other end.

"I want to speak to Nicola Tallant," he said in a northern accent.

"Speaking," I replied.

"The car at the Red Cow is purple," he said. "This is the Continuity IRA."

I had never taken a call from a terrorist organisation before, but I knew in the north during the time of The Troubles, they often rang into newsrooms and claimed responsibility for bombings and murders. I was almost sure there were codewords used, so every crank couldn't just claim them, but my man gave me none and arguing with him about the colour of the car at the Red Cow seemed pointless. Besides, who owns a purple car?

"This is the Continuity IRA and we missed Daniel. We missed Daniel at the Red Cow. We missed Daniel in Spain. We missed Daniel in the UK and we won't miss him the next time. We act on behalf of the entire Republican movement."

With that the call went dead. It was a strange one. The accent was funny and with no codeword I had no way of checking the validity of the call. I also thought it odd that the caller used the name 'Daniel' as if there was a familiarity, or that Kinahan had crossed that line that so few do by being so famous they are simply known by their first name.

Not long after the call there were more things to worry about and soundings were being made that a couple of journalists, myself included, might be issued with GIMs or Garda Information Messages, an official warning that there is a credible threat to life. The summit at the Byrne house had been hot headed and there was dangerous talk. Tensions were clearly at boiling point and the sense of unease hung in the air over the north inner-city where our offices were located, close to the heartland of Hutch territory.

At Raleigh Square, visitors continued to arrive at the Byrnes' home to offer condolences. Our team spotted Bomber along with several associates, while Freddie Thompson, who'd flown in from Spain, also called to commiserate with his aunt and uncle and to throw his weight behind the threat of revenge.

I was glad to finish up that day and head for home. On my way, I noticed there were already a few checkpoints on the road showing how gardai were acting reactively to the immediate threat. I knew it wouldn't be long before the mafia sought out their brutal revenge and I could only hope that no journalist, garda or any other innocent person would be targeted.

The following afternoon I was presented with the GIM form – a white piece of paper telling me that there was a threat to my life.

"An Garda Siochana are in possession of information relating to a likely threat to cause serious harm to you. The threat is said to arise from your ongoing reporting concerning two rival organised crime gangs," it read.

Twenty years since Veronica Guerin was murdered it seemed that a criminal gang had forgotten the tsunami of law enforcement that came for them in the wake of her killing, and were again blaming the messenger.

As a new week began the Regency stayed right at the top of every news bulletin, but the story became focused on the weigh-in and why journalists were there, but no gardai. The criticism was fierce and the situation undoubtedly looked bad. Hotel owner James McGettigan took to the airwaves to say he had tried to raise the alarm three times, but his calls went unanswered.

He had witnessed the murder: "He was shot three times, twice in the body and once in the head. These guys made sure he was killed. There was smoke coming out of his body."

He said he couldn't get through to gardai on 999 and had eventually phoned an officer he knew. It struck me that the Regency was the same hotel the Kinahan brothers had booked following the funeral of their mother the year previous, and its location, close to the airport, clearly suited them as a venue